AQA PSYCHOLOGY
A LEVEL PAPER THREE
SCHIZOPHRENIA

The *Extending Knowledge and Skills* series is a fresh approach to A Level Psychology, designed for the greater demands of the new AQA specification and assessment, and especially written to stretch and challenge students aiming for higher grades.

Dealing with the optional topic of AQA's **Paper 3: Schizophrenia**, this book is deliberately laid out with the assessment objectives in mind, from **AO1: Knowledge and understanding material**, followed by **AO2: Application material**, to **AO3: Evaluation and analysis material**. Providing the most in-depth, accessible coverage available of individual topics in Paper 3, the text is packed full of pedagogical features, including:

- **Question time** features to ensure that the reader is consistently challenged throughout the book.
- **New research** sections clearly distinguished within each chapter to ensure readers have access to cutting-edge material.
- A clear focus on the **assessment objectives** for the Paper topic to ensure readers know when and where to apply knowledge.
- The use of **example answers with examiner-style comments** to provide greater insight into how to/how not to answer exam questions.

An engaging, relevant and challenging text that broadens student understanding beyond that of the average textbook, this is the essential companion for any student taking the AQA A Level Paper 3 in Psychology.

Phil Gorman is an experienced psychology teacher and Assistant Principal Examiner for Paper 3 of the AQA A Level Psychology specification. He has been teaching this subject at A Level for over 25 years and examining for roughly the same amount of time. His examining experience has, in the past, taken him to the position of Chief Examiner for Edexcel A Level Psychology.

T0246235

Extending Knowledge and Skills Series

The *Extending Knowledge and Skills Series* is a fresh approach to A Level psychology, designed for greater demands of the new AQA specification and assessment, and especially written to stretch and challenge students aiming for higher grades.

Going beyond the reach of traditional revision textbooks, each book in the series provides wider explanations and greater levels of detail on each of the main topics within each paper option and shows how to apply this knowledge in an exam setting to produce higher tier responses.

Books in the Series:

AQA Psychology A Level Paper Three: Issues and Debates
Phil Gorman

AQA Psychology A Level Paper Three: Relationships
Phil Gorman

AQA Psychology A Level Paper Three: Schizophrenia
Phil Gorman

AQA Psychology A Level Paper Three: Forensic Psychology
Phil Gorman

AQA Psychology A Level Paper Three

Schizophrenia

Phil Gorman

Routledge
Taylor & Francis Group

LONDON AND NEW YORK

First published 2020
by Routledge
2 Park Square, Milton Park, Abingdon, Oxon OX14 4RN

and by Routledge
52 Vanderbilt Avenue, New York, NY 10017

Routledge is an imprint of the Taylor & Francis Group, an informa business

© 2020 Phil Gorman

British Library Cataloguing-in-Publication Data
A catalogue record for this book is available from the British Library

Library of Congress Cataloging-in-Publication Data
A catalog record has been requested for this book

ISBN: 978-0-367-40388-1 (hbk)
ISBN: 978-0-367-40387-4 (pbk)
ISBN: 978-0-429-35582-0 (ebk)

Typeset in Goudy Old Style and Frutiger
by Servis Filmsetting Ltd, Stockport, Cheshire

It is only in the mysterious equations of love that any logic or reason can be found.

(John Nash, 1994)

For my wife Debbie. No logic, no reason, I just love your mysterious ways.

Contents

Illustrations

Figures

Table

Chapter 1
Introduction

The aims of this book

This book is intended for A Level Psychology students studying the AQA syllabus and has been developed in order to provide further elaboration for the main Paper 3 topics. This particular book will deal with the optional topic of Schizophrenia from section C of Paper 3.

The book has been deliberately laid out with the assessment objectives in mind, so you will find AO1 – Knowledge and Understanding material first, followed by AO2 – Application material, and then AO3 – Evaluation and analysis material.

Each of the assessment objectives will have an injunction/command word or some other indication that will give you an idea of the particular objective being assessed and how you are supposed to answer the question.

AO1 will include some of the following injunctions/commands words that will indicate you are required to show knowledge and understanding:

Compare – identify similarities and differences.
Identify – Name or state what it is.
Name – Identify using a technical term.
Describe – Provide an account of.
Distinguish – Explain how two things differ.
Explain – Show what the purpose or reason for something is.
Give – Provide an answer from memory or from the information shown.
Outline – Provide the main characteristics.
State – Clearly set out.
What is meant by – Provide a definition.

AO2 will open with some kind of stem, which might be in the form of some information that you will need to refer to in your answer. For example:

Question 1

Studies have shown a relationship between early childhood trauma and the development of the positive symptoms of schizophrenia, particularly hallucinations. However, no such link has been found for the negative symptoms such as avolition.

Explain these findings with reference to the influence of both nature and nurture on schizophrenia?

Alternatively, AO2 questions may provide a description of a scenario with the names of some fictional character(s) who are involved in a situation that is relevant to an area of psychology. You could then be asked to explain this situation using knowledge derived from the relevant topic.

Question 2

Ricardo was born on the Caribbean island of Hispaniola but is now living in Britain. He has recently been having some problems with his doctor who he feels is trying to hurt him with the medication the doctor has been trying to get him to take. The doctor seems to be concerned about Ricardo saying that he is able to speak to dead relatives, but Ricardo can't understand why that is a problem.

Explain why Ricardo may have been given a diagnosis of schizophrenia by the doctor. How might cultural bias have affected this diagnosis?

Questions with a stem like this, which then ask you to refer to the stem in some way, are looking to assess AO2, so you need to ensure that you make clear reference to the stem by using some of the information as part of your answer. You will see examples of these in the coming chapters with some sample answers to show you how to deal with them.

AO3 will include some of the following injunctions/commands words that will indicate you are required to demonstrate skills of analysis and evaluation.

Discuss – Present strengths and weaknesses of a topic (in 16-mark questions, this can also require some element of description and can be taken as similar to describe and evaluate).

Evaluate – Make a judgement about a topic with reference to evidence.

One of the important features of this book and other books in the series is that there is a clear emphasis on the kind of skills required for the A Level Psychology exam, so the plenary sections use questions that are focused on exam skills and, at the end of every chapter, there are some exam-style questions with advice on how to answer them and examples of the kinds of answers that could be given to gain very high marks. Key words will be presented in bold and placed in a glossary at the end of each chapter, to make it easier to follow what these words mean and be able to use them more readily yourself.

Further features include an emphasis on new research that is both up to date and challenging, so there will be topics that don't just follow the usual pattern but will make you think again about the kinds of topics that you are studying.

The book also uses the technique of interleaving by bringing back topics from earlier studies to reinforce and consolidate earlier learning. All too often topics that have been studied earlier can be forgotten and it has been shown that by regularly revisiting these topics, it is possible to remember much more easily than by simply trying to cram them all in at the end.

What is mental health?

Mental health is as important as physical health for our feeling of well-being and stability, it includes a range of social, psychological and emotional factors that have an enormous effect on our daily lives and can either help or hinder our ability to function at work, within our families and in our relationships with friends or loved ones.

Unfortunately, when people talk about their health, they all too often are talking about their physical health without enough recognition being given to mental health. However, when you ask someone how they are (as we often do), they will often refer to factors that are closely related to their mental health, even if they don't immediately recognise it. People might say things like 'not too bad, but I do feel a bit run down today' or 'I'm OK, just got a bit of a headache', etc. Many of the symptoms that someone might put down to their physical health could just as well be related to their mental health.

These are some of the signs that someone might be suffering problems with their mental health:

- Problems with sleeping.
- A change in eating habits (could be eating more or less).
- An increase in smoking, drinking or drug-taking.
- A loss of energy and motivation or feeling like nothing matters.
- Withdrawing from usual activities.
- Having severe mood swings from very high to very low.
- Experiencing unexplained aches and pains.
- Having persistent thoughts, particularly about things that aren't true or hearing or seeing things that aren't there.
- Having fights or serious disagreements with people or thinking of harming yourself or others.
- Feeling confused, angry, upset, scared or very forgetful.

Why do we study schizophrenia?

Having taught the topic of schizophrenia many times over the last couple of decades, I can remember introducing the topic to one group of students in a very typical way, by getting them to tell me the first five words that come into their heads when they heard the word schizophrenia. I was expecting some of the usual confusion that surrounds this subject with possibly some suggesting that it involved having multiple personalities, which of course it does not. However, when I asked the first student for their first word, what they said was *murder*! I was taken aback by this initially, but I quickly realised that I should not be, as one of the most common misconceptions about the disorder is that it makes people violent, aggressive or dangerous. This view of the disorder is perpetuated by the media, with stories about individuals who have attacked someone because voices in their head told them to, and with the film industry regularly turning out films that depict people with schizophrenia as crazed murderers, wandering our streets, just waiting to attack us for no apparent reason.

If we are able to understand the condition of schizophrenia better and have a better understanding of those with the disorder, then this should mean that we can respond better when we meet or hear about people suffering with the condition.

What is covered in the Schizophrenia topic?

The topic considers three main questions that are of interest to anyone looking at a mental disorder:

- How do we know if someone has it?
- What causes it?
- How can it be treated?

These three questions are developed by looking at the **classification and diagnosis of schizophrenia**, the **biological and psychological explanations** and the **biological and psychological treatments,** with an extra consideration of taking an **interactionist approach** that combines both biological and psychological factors.

The first of these areas to be developed, classification and diagnosis, concerns what it is, and this is something that continues to cause confusion and misunderstanding from all sectors, professional and non-professional alike.

Activity 1

Try to answer the question above that I posed for my students and write down the first five words that come to mind when you hear the word schizophrenia (please don't say murder!).

1. _____
2. _____
3. _____
4. _____
5. _____

New research

S. Guloksuz and J. Van Os (2018) The slow death of the concept of schizophrenia and the painful birth of the psychosis spectrum. Psychological Medicine, 48 (2), pp. 229–244.

In this review article, the authors argue that, even though the concept of schizophrenia has always been contested, it has remained in use, at least partly, because it has been part of the 'psychiatric tradition', which has helped to provide a sense of identity for those working in the profession. However, they argue that it is more and more coming to be seen as a problem for those working in the profession, particularly as other disorders are now being seen as existing on a spectrum, e.g. autism spectrum disorder.

They argue that this means it is not possible to simply argue that we can make a distinction between those that have schizophrenia and those that do not, but instead we should consider the disorder as existing on a spectrum along which all members of the population vary. Therefore, if we take the example of the most common symptoms, hallucinations and delusions, we cannot say that if you have either of these then you are suffering with schizophrenia because people may suffer with them to varying degrees and some of these people may be suffering with schizophrenia and some not.

They believe that in order to provide a proper diagnosis and classification of the disorder, we must have an understanding of the subtleties of psychotic symptoms and an awareness that it is very difficult to provide a broad distinction between those with and without the disorder unless we are able to recognise these subtleties. This is particularly true due to the low levels of agreement between professionals as to what constitutes schizophrenia and what does not!

Question time

What does this research tell us about how easy it is to diagnose someone with schizophrenia?

What does this say about the rest of the population?

Should you reconsider the five words you came up with previously? Why? How?

Explanations of schizophrenia

Once you have decided what schizophrenia is, it is a good idea to try to figure out what causes it. The explanations tend to be divided between the biological, focusing on genes, neurochemicals and brain structure, and the psychological, focusing on family dysfunction and cognitive processes.

The explanation for any behaviour is always hotly disputed and this is nowhere more true than in the study of mental disorders. Many will argue that the best way to understand schizophrenia is with reference to biology as this provides us with the most convenient method of treatment, however, others will argue that the disorder is far too complex to be reduced to simple biological factors and look for explanations in life events or the depths of the mind.

Activity 2

Consider the factors mentioned above as part of the biological and psychological explanations and try to explain what each of them might say about the development of schizophrenia in the table below.

Factors related to the cause of schizophrenia	Possible explanations
Genes	
Neurochemistry	
Brain structure	
Family dysfunction	
Cognitive processes	

Question time

Which of these factors do you think provides the best explanation?

Is it possible to accept just one or would it be beneficial to take an interactionist approach?

Treatments for schizophrenia

Probably the most important thing about the study of schizophrenia is what we can do once we have figured out what causes it. Indeed, it is usually the case that once we have figured out the cause, this in itself provides us with important information as to how we can treat it.

Inevitably, due to the factors identified above, the treatments for schizophrenia tend to be divided between those that focus on the use of biological approaches and those that focus on psychological approaches. The main biological approach being medication to treat the supposed biological imbalances and the main psychological approach being some form of therapy to either change the way of thinking of the disordered individual or to change their living situation, which might help them to recover.

Activity 3

Sid has been diagnosed with schizophrenia and is currently receiving antipsychotic medication, which helps to keep him calm. Sid's doctors believe that this is the best way to keep Sid calm and free from the most disturbing symptoms of the disorder – alarming hallucinations involving a voice that says dreadful things about Sid, which then cause Sid to become extremely angry.

Sid's family have spoken to some other doctors who believe that he would be better treated by the use of psychological therapies to get to the root cause of Sid's problems. This would mean that the problems could be dealt with once and for all. However, Sid's current doctors think that he wouldn't benefit from this approach as, without the medication, Sid's grip on reality is problematic, making it difficult for him to cope without it.

Who do you think is right? Should Sid's family keep him on the medication or follow the psychotherapy route? Is there another way?

New research

Help guide

Schizophrenia treatment and self-help

Melinda Smith, Lawrence Robinson and Jeanne Segal

https://www.helpguide.org/articles/mental-disorders/schizophrenia-treatment-and-self-help.htm (accessed 1 November, 2019)

The article outlines how early diagnosis and treatment can be particularly helpful but also focuses on the use of self-help to provide a better possibility of leading a normal life for those diagnosed.

The authors want to show that the pessimistic view of schizophrenia being life-long with no hope of recovery is wrong and offer advice on how to deal with it.

They try to make a few points very clear:

- **Schizophrenia can be treated**. Although there is no cure for schizophrenia, it can still be managed.
- **People with schizophrenia can have a normal life**. The right treatment can ensure that people with schizophrenia are able to live a normal life, including work and relationships, in the same way as anyone else.
- **Being diagnosed doesn't mean spending long periods in hospital**. The right support can avoid the need for hospitalisation.
- **Most people will improve**. Out of every five people with the disorder, only one will continue to have the same symptoms long-term.

One of the more surprising comments about treatment comes from the fact that the authors put a lot of emphasis on diet and exercise for the management of the disorder. They argue that regular activity can help to keep you calm and that focusing on how your body feels when you are moving, e.g. how your feet feel when they hit the floor can help to take your mind away from other thoughts.

They further argue that eating a balanced and nutritious diet can help to avoid frequent changes in blood sugar levels, which can have an effect on mood if left uncontrolled. This means that mood swings can be avoided, which can be particularly beneficial if accompanied by an avoidance of other chemicals such as alcohol or illegal drugs.

Question time

What does this article tell us about the treatment of schizophrenia?

Do you think that diet and exercise can have an effect on the symptoms?

Is there anything else that people diagnosed with schizophrenia should do?

Summary

This introduction should have got you ready for more of this kind of discussion and will hopefully aid you in your further understanding of these fascinating topics.

Chapter 2
Classification and diagnosis of schizophrenia

Spec check

Classification of schizophrenia. Positive symptoms of schizophrenia, including hallucinations and delusions. Negative symptoms of schizophrenia, including speech poverty and avolition.

Reliability and validity in diagnosis and classification of schizophrenia including reference to comorbidity, culture and gender bias and symptom overlap.

AO1 (Knowledge and understanding): The classification and diagnosis of schizophrenia

What is schizophrenia?

- Schizophrenia is a disorder that affects around one per cent of the world's population, although this figure varies from country to country and can be much lower in some places.
- It is more common in males than in females, with a ratio of about 1.4:1.
- It is more common among people with ages ranging from late teens to early thirties.
- It is more common in working-class than middle-class people and in urban rather than rural areas.

In the introduction to this volume, I talked about some of the problems with the perception of schizophrenia and how and why people become confused about what constitutes the disorder. As was suggested previously, this isn't exactly helped by the media who perpetuate the view of a person with schizophrenia as someone who is violently out of control. However, it should be noted that even without the intervention of the media, there has long been a misunderstanding of the disorder, partially due to the fact that people with the disorder aren't always in touch with reality and will see things, hear things and believe things that other people simply do not. The disorder is often viewed quite differently from other mental disorders because of this, and anecdotally it has often been suggested that 'talking to yourself is the first sign of madness'. As someone with schizophrenia may well respond to voices in their head that no one else can see or hear, it's not totally surprising that people with schizophrenia are seen in this way.

> **Think!**
>
> Are the media responsible for the negative view of schizophrenia?
>
> Is talking to yourself a sign of madness?
>
> Do we need to change our view of people with schizophrenia?

Classification and diagnosis of schizophrenia

Possibly the best way to change people's view of schizophrenia and to dispel the myths associated with the disorder is to consider the official classification of the disorder from those involved in its diagnosis. According to Aggarwal et al. (2015) the classification of a disorder is concerned with the general features that can be applied to most people within that category, whereas the diagnosis is concerned with the signs and symptoms that can help to guide the care of an individual patient. The two main organisations involved in this process in the UK are the World Health Organisation (WHO), which publishes the *International Classification of Diseases* (ICD), and the American Psychiatric Association, which publishes the *Diagnostic and Statistical Manual of Mental Disorders* (DSM). These two publications help to prevent individual, subjective descriptions of mental disorders by providing set criteria that can be used by everyone as the basis for understanding and differentiating between those that have a particular disorder and those that have something else, or no disorder at all, both of them provide both classification and diagnostic criteria.

ICD and DSM classification systems

The ICD-11 (2018, the 11th edition) is used across most countries in the world as it covers more than just mental disorders and is actually the officially recognised system for diagnosing mental disorders in the US, although not all psychiatrists in the US are aware of this. The DSM-5 is the *main* classification system used in the US, although it is also used in the UK and most other parts of the world and has become the benchmark for doctors and psychiatrists diagnosing those with mental disorders.

ICD-11

The ICD-11 is the most recent edition of this classification system and while it previously had a range of sub-types of schizophrenia (that were meant to be quite different from one another), it has moved to a new approach involving a system of descriptors with a rating scale for each to identify the severity of the disorder. The descriptors are based around the idea of positive symptoms such as delusions, hallucinations, experiences of passivity and control, and disorganised thinking and behaviour as well as negative symptoms such as reductions in emotion, speech, motivation and social interaction in a similar way as before but also includes a number of other descriptors.

In terms of diagnosis, ICD-11 says:

> The normal requirement for a diagnosis of schizophrenia requires the presence of at least 2 out of 8 symptoms, including at least one core symptom. Core symptoms include positive symptoms such as delusions and hallucinations. Symptoms should have been clearly present for most of the time during a period of at least 1 month.

DSM-5

This new edition of the DSM has made some changes to how schizophrenia is classified, with one of the major changes being that the subtypes have been removed and replaced with a more general title of schizophrenia spectrum. This reflects some of the problems encountered in trying to differentiate between different types and in particular the problems associated with the subtype of catatonic schizophrenia.

In terms of diagnosis, DSM-5 says:

> The presence of 2 (or more) of the following, each present for a significant portion of time, with at least 1 of them being (1), (2), or (3): (1) delusions, (2) hallucinations, (3) disorganized speech, (4) grossly disorganized or catatonic behavior, and (5) negative symptoms.
>
> (APA, DSM-5, 2013).

Both systems have recognised the need to remove the sub-types from their classification which previously caused problems in terms of the validity of the diagnosis. Both focus on the need for symptoms to be present for one month, although the DSM requires some level of disturbance to be present over a period of six months.

Question time

What are the similarities and differences between the ICD-11 and DSM-5 in terms of the classification and diagnosis of schizophrenia?

What do you think the problems might be in having two different systems operating at the same time?

The difference between positive and negative symptoms

Schizophrenia is often described as having both positive symptoms and negative symptoms, which is not to say that some are good and some are bad, but is in fact using the terms positive and negative in a way that indicates that something has been added or taken away. The term positive is being used to explain that they are things that someone with schizophrenia has added to their normal abilities, e.g. hearing voices that aren't there, whereas negative is being used to explain things that are taken away from their normal abilities, e.g. lack of speech.

Positive symptoms

The two main positive symptoms listed in both the ICD-11 and DSM-5 are hallucinations and delusions.

Hallucinations are sensory experiences that only exist inside the mind of the person who is experiencing them and are not experienced by anyone else. The most common form of hallucination for a person suffering with schizophrenia is to hear voices in their heads that appear to be coming from some other person(s). The voices will often provide a commentary on the sufferer's life, e.g. she is opening the door, and as such can be neutral, although they may be complimentary or critical and will often cause significant distress to the individual. Hallucinations can affect any of the senses and the sufferer may also see or smell things that aren't there.

Delusions are beliefs in things that are not true and, for the person with schizophrenia, these will often involve beliefs about who they are, what they can do and what other people might do to them. The delusions about who they are can give rise to feelings of grandeur as they may believe themselves to be an important historical figure. The delusions about what they can do can relate to their ability to be in control of certain things. For example, they may believe they have control over things that they don't, such as the weather; or that they have no control over things that they do, such as their own limbs. The delusions about what other people might do to them can be experienced as paranoia, if they believe that others are going to hurt or persecute them.

The two main negative symptoms are speech poverty and avolition.

Speech poverty or alogia is characterised by a reduction in speech and apparent blockages in the production of speech. Sufferers will find it difficult to respond with more than just a few basic utterances and will often confine themselves to slow, monosyllabic responses to questions.

Avolition or apathy is shown by the inability of the sufferer to engage in activity that might result in them achieving some desired goal. The sufferer will appear to have a lack of energy and lack the motivation to complete activities related to personal hygiene and grooming and will also lack the persistence to keep up with work or educational matters.

Think!

Are the symptoms outlined above the characteristics that you would expect to find in someone with schizophrenia?

Are these characteristics present in any other people who do not have schizophrenia?

Mini plenary

Without referring back to the text, provide definitions of the following terms:

- Classification   _____
- Diagnosis   _____
- ICD-11   _____
- DSM-5   _____
- Positive symptoms   _____
- Negative symptoms _____

AO2 (Application of knowledge): How does this apply in practice?

Interleave me now

Gender bias in diagnosis

As previously mentioned, there is a difference in the diagnosis of schizophrenia in that it seems to affect males more commonly than females. This is an issue, because it is necessary to consider the reasons for this difference and, specifically, whether this is just a coincidental factor or whether some bias in the diagnostic process is causing this difference to occur.

Forms of gender bias

Androcentrism is the tendency to focus attention on males at the expense of females.

Alpha bias overplays the importance of gender in our understanding of human behaviour and suggests that men and women are completely different. Either implicitly, or sometimes explicitly, it suggests that the behaviour of the two should be explained quite differently.

Beta bias downplays the importance of gender in our understanding of human behaviour and suggests (as above) that we can ignore the issue of gender, as men and women are basically the same and, therefore, we can just study men if we wish and apply the results to women.

We need to consider how these forms of bias may manifest themselves in relation to the diagnosis of schizophrenia.

Androcentrism: In a review of studies into the incidence of schizophrenia, Longenecker et al. (2010) found that since the 1980s the number of men appearing in studies outnumbered women in a ratio of 1.4:1, which could be explained by the higher incidence of schizophrenia in men or by the increased focus on men in these studies, or possibly by a tendency to focus diagnosis more on males than on females.

Alpha bias: Research into the early diagnosis of schizophrenia by Høye et al. (2006) questioned 467 psychiatrists in Norway and Russia and gave them the same description of a patient with symptoms that could be interpreted as schizophrenia. The only difference was that the gender was changed, so that half of the psychiatrists received a male version and half a female version of the diagnosis. They found that the 'male' patients were significantly more likely to be given a diagnosis of schizophrenia than the 'female' patients, suggesting that clinicians are overemphasising the differences between the genders in their diagnoses.

Beta bias: Falkenburg and Tracy (2012) have identified a number of factors that may be responsible for the differences in the incidence of schizophrenia in males and females, including the 'oestrogen hypothesis', which suggests that the female hormone may have protective effects. They also suggest other social factors, such as lower familial engagement in men and lower socioeconomic status in women, that may explain why men suffer more negative symptoms and also that the positive symptoms differ in content between the genders. Ignoring these differences may have important implications for the treatment of the disorder.

Think!

What does this tell us about the incidence of schizophrenia in men and women? Why do you think this bias occurs?

Are there any other factors that may explain why men are more likely to be diagnosed with schizophrenia than women?

Interleave me now

Cultural bias in diagnosis

The incidence of schizophrenia is also different for people from different countries and for those from different cultures within the same country. This seems to suggest that there are more than biological factors involved in schizophrenia, and that the diagnosis of the disorder may also be affected by cultural factors. These factors could be related to the behaviour of different groups or could be related to bias on the part of the clinicians making the diagnosis.

Forms of cultural bias

Universality would suggest that it is possible to apply the findings of psychological research to everyone regardless of their apparent differences.

Ethnocentrism is the tendency to focus attention on your own culture or ethnic group at the expense of other cultures and ethnic groups.

An alternative to this approach would be **cultural relativism**, which involves accepting that cultural norms and values are different and that it is not possible to create a universal set of laws or rules that apply to everyone regardless of culture; and that doing so would fall into the trap of ethnocentrism.

In order to apply cultural bias to the diagnosis of schizophrenia, we need to consider how these forms of bias manifest themselves in relation to the diagnosis of schizophrenia.

Fearon et al. (2006) have reported that African Caribbean people resident in the UK are nine times more likely to be diagnosed with schizophrenia than their white counterparts, suggesting that there is something about being of African Caribbean origin in Britain that leads to a higher incidence of being diagnosed with schizophrenia. This is unlikely to be due to biological factors and as such points to some level of cultural bias operating amongst clinicians.

Universality: Fernando (2014) has argued that these differential diagnostic rates of schizophrenia are influenced by the category fallacy in which Western definitions of mental illness are inappropriately applied to non-Western cultures – suggesting that a universal approach may be inappropriate as it shows a lack of understanding of the relative cultural differences between ethnic groups.

Ethnocentrism: This tendency is also supported by Whaley (2004) who believed that the differences in the incidence of schizophrenia between black Americans (2.1 per cent) and white Americans (1.4 per cent) was due to ethnic differences being overlooked by predominantly white practitioners, particularly in relation to the issue of paranoia, whereby mistrust of white doctors is misinterpreted as a symptom of schizophrenia.

Question time

What do gender and culture bias tell us about the diagnosis of schizophrenia?

Do the classification and diagnostic systems make diagnosis less likely to be biased?

How could the diagnosis be improved?

Mini plenary

Ricardo was born on the Caribbean island of Hispaniola but is now living in Britain. He has recently been having some problems with his doctor. Ricardo believes his doctor is trying to hurt him with the medication being prescribed. The doctor is concerned that Ricardo is saying that he is able to speak to dead relatives, but Ricardo cannot understand why that is a problem.

Explain why Ricardo may have been given a diagnosis of schizophrenia by the doctor. How might cultural bias have affected this diagnosis?

AO3 (Analysis and evaluation of knowledge): How useful is this approach to classification and diagnosis?

Why might a diagnosis of schizophrenia not be reliable?

In order to be classed as reliable a diagnosis of schizophrenia should be consistent, so if one clinician diagnoses someone with the disorder, then another clinician faced with the same patient should give the same diagnosis. This is called inter-rater reliability and measures the extent to which clinicians agree on the diagnosis of patients with the same symptoms.

One of the problems with providing a consistent diagnosis is that there is more than one classification and diagnostic system in use at the same time (DSM-5 and ICD-11), and they use slightly different criteria for making a diagnosis. This makes it almost inevitable that the diagnosis provided is unlikely to be consistent. If one clinician is judging a patient using the DSM and another using the ICD, then it is quite likely that they will come up with a different diagnosis depending on the symptoms presented.

In an attempt to overcome this problem, Cheniaux et al. (2009) got two psychiatrists to diagnose 100 volunteer in-patients from a Brazilian psychiatric institute who were suffering with a range of disorders, using both the DSM and ICD criteria. This would mean that both the reliability of each system could be compared, to see if the different criteria produced the same diagnosis, as well as the inter-rater reliability of each clinician using the same criteria. The results were that one psychiatrist diagnosed 26 with schizophrenia using DSM and 44 using ICD and the other diagnosed 13 using DSM and 24 using ICD.

This shows that neither the two systems nor the two psychiatrists were consistent in their diagnoses of the patients, suggesting that there is a reliability problem with the diagnosis of schizophrenia and, as such, it is hard to obtain a diagnosis for schizophrenia on which everyone can agree. However, it should be noted that the main finding of this research was that ICD produced a significantly higher number of diagnoses of schizophrenia than did DSM, which the researchers concluded was due to the less restrictive criteria of ICD, for example one month duration compared to six months for DSM, and the fact that negative symptoms alone were enough for a diagnosis in ICD (using the old ICD-10) but not in DSM. Apart from this higher incidence, the level of inter-rater reliability for the two psychiatrists was correlated as higher than 0.5, which is still not significant enough but slightly higher than the raw data alone would suggest.

Why might the diagnosis of schizophrenia not be valid?

In the Cheniaux study above, the two psychiatrists were not merely being asked to diagnose patients with schizophrenia, they were also being asked to decide which disorder each of the patients was suffering with from a list of possible disorders, which included schizoaffective disorder, bipolar disorder and unipolar depression. In order to do this, the psychiatrists would have to be able to distinguish one disorder from another by analysing the symptoms of each. This kind of descriptive validity provides a measure of the extent to which the criteria for each disorder are different enough to be able to provide an accurate diagnosis.

The findings outlined above indicated that more patients were being diagnosed with schizophrenia using the ICD system than the DSM, suggesting that a number of patients diagnosed with schizophrenia by ICD were being diagnosed with something else using DSM. The main culprit for the other diagnoses in the study was schizoaffective disorder that had the lowest levels of inter-rater reliability; the number of diagnoses given to this disorder was close to the number of differences found between the diagnoses for schizophrenia using the two systems. Schizoaffective disorder has a number of symptoms that are very similar to schizophrenia and as such it may be difficult to provide a clearly distinct diagnosis from that of schizophrenia.

This suggests that it is not easy to provide a clearly separate diagnosis of schizophrenia and that clinicians may not be able to distinguish between one disorder and another using either or both of the classification systems. Consequently, we cannot say that the diagnosis of schizophrenia is an entirely valid one.

How does comorbidity create problems in the diagnosis of schizophrenia?

Comorbidity refers to the possibility that a patient may be suffering with more than one condition at the same time, which makes it hard to distinguish between the two and causes problems with the validity of the diagnosis. It may be unclear which is which, and also whether there are more disorders present at all. This could be an issue for schizophrenia, as it calls into question whether it actually exists as a separate disorder as well as potentially causing problems for the treatment of patients, as it may be unclear what needs to be treated.

In a review of studies, Buckley et al. (2009) found that there were high levels of comorbid psychiatric conditions among patients with schizophrenia, particularly in the areas of depression, substance abuse and anxiety. They found that comorbid depression occurs in about 50 per cent of cases, 47 per cent of patients also have a lifetime diagnosis of comorbid substance abuse with 29 per cent also suffering with PTSD and 23 per cent with comorbid obsessive compulsive disorder (OCD).

This is a very confusing picture. It makes it unclear whether these disorders constitute completely separate disorders not connected to schizophrenia, which merely occur by chance, or whether they are part of a possible subcategory of schizophrenia and require further analysis. They even bring into question whether our understanding of schizophrenia is completely wrong and the whole classification needs to be completely rethought. Furthermore, if the diagnosis of schizophrenia is wrong, this brings into question the treatment of the disorder and whether the disorder is being worsened by the treatment or may indeed be leading to further complications or comorbid conditions.

Buckley et al. were interested in exactly these sorts of questions. They came to the conclusion that there was little evidence from the data to suggest that these conditions were anything more than coincidentally occurring in people with schizophrenia, but that the presence of comorbid conditions did cause deeper problems and the length of time that they suffered with schizophrenia to be extended. The exception to this was the incidence of OCD, which they argued could be seen as a 'schizo-obsessive' subtype of schizophrenia as opposed to simply comorbid. This was important as they also argued that it may have a different response to treatment and that simply regarding it as comorbid and treating it accordingly may actually make the condition worse.

This all suggests that comorbidity makes it more difficult to provide a reliable and valid diagnosis of schizophrenia, which may bring into question the predictive validity of the diagnosis and cause significant problems for the treatment of those suffering with the disorder.

What is the problem with symptom overlap?

Both the DSM and ICD identify sets of symptoms for different mental disorders, which provide clinicians with the criteria they need to be able to identify accurately the particular condition that is affecting an individual patient. This works best when the symptoms for each disorder are completely different, so it is possible to say, for example, that if someone has bizarre delusions then they definitely have schizophrenia. Unfortunately, it isn't quite that simple, and it is often the case that some of the symptoms of one disorder can also be found in the list of symptoms for another disorder. An obvious example of this is in the overlap between schizophrenia and schizoaffective disorder referred to earlier.

However, schizoaffective disorder is not the only disorder where this problem of symptom overlap occurs. A number of other disorders have some symptoms that appear in the classification system for schizophrenia, e.g. bipolar disorder, autism and dissociative identity disorder (DID), also known as multiple personality disorder.

One of the most common mistakes that people make when trying to explain what schizophrenia is like is to suggest that it involves having a split personality and therefore being Jack one minute and Jill the next. This mistake often occurs because of the delusional aspect of schizophrenia in which sufferers may, for example, believe themselves to be someone of great importance. This is a mistake, however, and the disorder that actually involves having more than one personality is multiple personality disorder (dissociative identity disorder).

However, Foote and Park (2008) have suggested that there may be both symptom and cause overlap in the two disorders, making it understandable that the two can be mistaken by clinicians as well as by the general public. This problem can particularly occur in the early stages of DID, whereby the voices of the different personalities 'leak through' and may begin to comment on events or even talk to the core personality without completely taking over. According to Foote and Park, this can lead to mistakes in diagnosis as the traditional diagnosis of hearing voices is that the individual is suffering with schizophrenia.

This kind of problem can also occur with bipolar disorder where the manic and depressive symptoms can sometimes appear very similar to the positive and negative symptoms of schizophrenia leading to an incorrect diagnosis and the resulting incorrect treatment.

Mini plenary

Using the evaluation points above, try to evaluate the following statement.

It's impossible to get an accurate diagnosis of schizophrenia.

Arguments for	Arguments against

A modern issue: do we still need the sub-types of schizophrenia?

19

In the new versions of the DSM and ICD classifications for schizophrenia, the sub-types were done away with. It is questionable whether they should have been removed. The article below attempts to explain why the subtypes were removed from DSM-5.

New research

MEDICAL NEWS TODAY

What are the different types of schizophrenia and why are they no longer used?

Yvette Brazier

Monday, 24 April 2017

In the article, Brazier notes that, in the past, there were different subtypes of schizophrenia including:

- Catatonic schizophrenia
- Childhood onset schizophrenia
- Disorganised schizophrenia
- Paranoid schizophrenia

However, in 2013 the publication of DSM-5 changed all of that and brought the subtypes under a single heading of schizophrenia, which happened, according to the American Psychiatric Association, because these subtypes had low reliability and validity and weren't stable in terms of their diagnostic use.

For each of the four subtypes identified above, Brazier explains why there were specific problems with them.

Catatonic schizophrenia

This includes extremes of behaviour, for example excessive movements but also massively decreased movement whereby the person doesn't respond at all. However, it can occur in a number of other disorders and so it is now considered a specifier for schizophrenia, rather than a type of schizophrenia.

Childhood onset schizophrenia

Schizophrenia is a disorder that occurs in early adulthood in most cases but can occasionally occur in childhood at around the age of 10. However, as children can often experience hallucinations, it was believed to be misleading to have a separate type, and that there is simply a need to deal with schizophrenia when it does occur.

Disorganised schizophrenia, or hebephrenia

While it is true that schizophrenia sufferers have disorganised thinking and behaviour, and that this can sometimes lead to problems with personal hygiene and other simple daily activities, such as effectively communicating with people, having disorganised thinking and behaviour is no longer considered to be a subtype and should be seen as just a feature.

Paranoid schizophrenia

Paranoia can be a feature of the delusional aspect of schizophrenia as sufferers have false beliefs that others are out to kill them or at least do them harm. However, it is now considered to be just a feature of the symptom of delusions, rather than a separate subtype.

Question time

What does this article tell us about the types of schizophrenia?

Do you think it was helpful to remove the subtypes or do you think we should still have them?

Does the new system make it easier or harder to diagnose someone with schizophrenia?

Chapter plenary

1. What is schizophrenia?
2. What is meant by the term classification in relation to schizophrenia?
3. What is meant by the term diagnosis in relation to schizophrenia?
4. What are the similarities and differences between the ICD-11 classification system and DSM-5 classification system?
5. What is the difference between positive and negative symptoms in relation to schizophrenia?
6. What are the different forms of gender bias in psychology?
7. How does gender bias affect the diagnosis of schizophrenia?
8. What are the different forms of cultural bias in psychology?
9. How does cultural bias affect the diagnosis of schizophrenia?
10. Why might the diagnosis of schizophrenia not be reliable?
11. Why might the diagnosis of schizophrenia not be valid?
12. How might comorbidity create problems in the diagnosis of schizophrenia?
13. Why is there a problem with symptom overlap in the diagnosis of schizophrenia?
14. Do we still need the sub-types of schizophrenia?

Glossary

Key word	Definition
American Psychiatric Association	The main professional organisation of psychiatrists in the USA and the largest psychiatric organisation in the world.
Avolition	The inability to engage in activity that might result in them achieving some desired goal.
Category fallacy	Western definitions of mental illness are inappropriately applied to non-Western cultures.
Classification	A system used to identify the general features of a disorder that can apply to most people within that category.
Comorbidity	Another illness or disorder occurring at the same time as schizophrenia.
Delusions	Beliefs in something that isn't true, for the person with schizophrenia these will often involve beliefs about who they are, what they can do and what other people might do to them.
Descriptive validity	A measure of the extent to which the criteria for each disorder are different enough to be able to provide an accurate diagnosis.
Diagnosis	The signs and symptoms that can help to guide the care of an individual patient.
Hallucinations	Sensory experiences that only exist inside the mind of the person who is experiencing them and are not experienced by anyone else.
Inter-rater reliability	A measure of the extent to which two clinicians give the same diagnosis to the same symptoms.
Negative symptoms	Symptoms that are absent in those with schizophrenia but are features that most people do experience.
Positive symptoms	Symptoms that most people do not experience but are present in those with schizophrenia.
Predictive validity	A measure of the extent to which a diagnosis leads to successful treatment.
Specifier	An extension to a diagnosis to further clarify a disorder or illness. It allows for a more specific diagnosis to be made.
Speech poverty	A reduction in speech and apparent blockages in the production of speech.
Symptom overlap	Symptoms of schizophrenia that are the same as symptoms of some other disorder.

Key word	Definition
World Health Organisation (WHO)	An international organisation operating within the United Nations system that attempts to promote healthy living and take a lead in global health responses.

Plenary: Exam-style questions and answers with advisory comments

Question 1.

Explain the difference between positive symptoms and negative symptoms in schizophrenia? [2 marks]

Marks for this question: AO1 = 2

Advice: In a question like this, it's important to make sure you are outlining the difference, rather than just what the positive and negative symptoms are. Although you will still need to show an understanding of this to get both marks. There is no need to provide any analysis or evaluation as both of the marks are for AO1: Knowledge and understanding.

Possible answer: The difference is that positive symptoms add something to the person with schizophrenia as they are behaviours that most people don't experience, e.g. hallucinations, whereas negative symptoms take something away from the person with schizophrenia as they are behaviours that most people do experience but the person with schizophrenia does not, e.g. speech poverty.

Question 2.

Describe and evaluate the classification and diagnosis of schizophrenia. [16 marks]

Marks for this question: AO1 = 6 and AO3 = 10

Advice: This question is looking for both skills of knowledge and understanding and analysis and evaluation. As there are 6 marks for AO1 and 10 for AO3, there should be greater emphasis on the evaluation. However, all such extended writing questions are marked holistically and therefore it is important that the knowledge is accurate and detailed and that the evaluation is clear and effective.

Possible answer: Schizophrenia is a mental disorder that is characterised by the sufferer experiencing hallucinations and delusions. It has a worldwide incidence rate of around 1 per cent, and it affects men more than women, young more than old, and those who live in the city more than in the country. It is one of the most misunderstood mental disorders and it is often confused with multiple personality disorder, due to the symptom of delusions in which sufferers will sometimes feel that they are someone else, usually someone important.

The official classification of this disorder should help to clear up any confusion as it attempts to identify the general features of this disorder that could apply to most people with it and also provides guidelines for diagnosis, which are the signs and symptoms of a disorder that can help to guide the care and treatment of an individual with the disorder.

There are two systems operating in the UK, ICD-11, which is a system used by many clinicians worldwide and is operated by the World Health Organisation, and the DSM-5, which is the benchmark for mental health professionals and is published by the American Psychiatric Association, but is also used by clinicians in the UK.

Both systems identify the typical signs and symptoms of schizophrenia as (a) positive symptoms, which add something to the behaviour of the sufferer that most people don't have, e.g. hallucinations and delusions; and (b) negative symptoms that take away something from the behaviour of the sufferer, as they don't have some things that most people do have, e.g. speech poverty and avolition. There are some similarities and differences between the two systems, in that they have both recently done away with sub-types but the DSM suggests that symptoms should have been present for longer than is required by the ICD system.

One of the issues with the classification and diagnosis of schizophrenia concerns the reliability or consistency of the diagnoses given, particularly in relation to inter-rater reliability, which deals with the extent to which two clinicians presented with the same symptoms would provide the same diagnosis. This was tested by Cheniaux et al. by asking two psychiatrists to diagnose the same 100 patients using both the DSM and ICD systems. This investigation enabled them to find out if the psychiatrists would provide a consistent conclusion and also to test whether the two systems would produce the same diagnoses. They found that there was fairly low reliability, as one psychiatrist diagnosed 26 with schizophrenia using the DSM and 44 using ICD and the other diagnosed 13 using the DSM and 24 using ICD. This suggests a fairly low level of inter-rater reliability but, more importantly, it also suggests an even lower level of consistency between the two systems, as the ICD system diagnosed many more of the 100 patients with schizophrenia than did the DSM system.

The other problem identified by this study was one of validity and, in particular, the ability of the two systems to provide descriptive validity, which is the extent to which the criteria used for different disorders by the two systems are different enough to provide an accurate diagnosis. Apart from diagnosing the 100 patients with schizophrenia, Cheniaux also asked the psychiatrists to diagnose schizoaffective disorder, bipolar disorder and unipolar depression. The findings indicated that the psychiatrists found it hard to distinguish between schizoaffective disorder and schizophrenia, which might help to explain the large difference between the numbers diagnosed in the two systems. It seems as though the symptoms of schizoaffective disorder are so similar to the symptoms of schizophrenia that it makes it very difficult to distinguish between the two and therefore affects the validity of both.

Further problems with the diagnosis of schizophrenia arise from potential gender and culture bias on the part of the clinicians making the diagnosis.

One of the features of schizophrenia identified above is that there is a higher incidence in men than in women, which is something that Longenecker et al. noticed happening in research studies using current patients diagnosed with the disorder. Their findings seem to suggest that there is either some natural factor that is causing more men to be suffering with schizophrenia or that there is some form of gender bias that is causing more men to be diagnosed. This latter factor is supported by Høye et al. who asked 467 psychiatrists to diagnose a patient who had symptoms that could be interpreted as schizophrenia, but in half the cases they were identified as male and the other half as male. They found that when the patient was identified as male, they were significantly more likely to be given a diagnosis of schizophrenia than when they were identified as female, in spite of all other information being the same. This suggests that the apparent difference in the incidence of schizophrenia is more to do with bias on the part of clinicians than it is to do with any real difference in the susceptibility to schizophrenia of males and females.

This kind of bias may also extend to different cultural groups as it has been identified by Fearon et al. that African Caribbean people living in the UK are nine times more likely to be diagnosed with schizophrenia than their white counterparts, suggesting that there is something about the experience of being of African Caribbean origin in Britain that makes you more susceptible to being diagnosed with schizophrenia. Fernando argues that the problems arise from the category fallacy in which Western notions of normal behaviour are inappropriately applied to individuals from non-Western backgrounds, suggesting that the problem is a cultural one rather than a clinical one.

These issues suggest that the system of classifying and diagnosing schizophrenia is not entirely reliable or valid and that it is potentially subject to bias. This may have important implications for the treatment of schizophrenia both now and in the future because if we cannot be certain that the right diagnosis is being given, we cannot be certain that the right treatment is being given either.

References

Aggarwal, R., Ringold, S., Khanna, D., Neogi, T., Johnson, S. R., Miller, A., Brunner, H. I., Ogawa, R., Felson, D. (2015) Distinctions between diagnostic and classification criteria? Arthritis Care & Research, 67 (7): 891–897.

American Psychiatric Association (2013) Diagnostic and Statistical Manual of Mental Disorders, 5th edn. Washington, DC: APA, pp. 99–105.

Brazier, Y. (2017) What are the different types of schizophrenia? Medical News Today. https://www.medicalnewstoday.com/articles/192770 (accessed 19 November 2019).

Buckley, P.F., Miller, B.J., Lehrer, D.S. and Castle, D.J. (2009) Psychiatric comorbidities and schizophrenia. Schizophrenia Bulletin, 35 (2): 383–402.

Cheniaux, E., Landeira-Fernandez, J. and Versiani, M. (2009) The diagnoses of schizophrenia, schizoaffective disorder, bipolar disorder and unipolar depression: interrater reliability and congruence between DSM-IV and ICD-10. Psychopathology, 42 (5): 293–298.

Falkenburg, J. and Tracy, D.K. (2014). Sex and schizophrenia: A review of gender differences. *Psychosis*, 6 (1): 61–69.

Fearon, P., Kirkbride, J.B., Morgan, C., Dazzan, P., Morgan, K., Lloyd, T., Hutchinson, G., Tarrant, J., Fung, W.L.A., Holloway, J. and Mallett, R. (2006) Incidence of schizophrenia and other psychoses in ethnic minority groups: Results from the MRC AESOP Study. *Psychological Medicine*, 36 (11): 1541–1550.

Fernando, S. (2014) *Race and Culture in Psychiatry (Psychology Revivals)*. Oxford: Routledge.

Foote, B. and Park, J. (2008) Dissociative identity disorder and schizophrenia: Differential diagnosis and theoretical issues. *Current Psychiatry Reports*, 10 (3): 217.

Høye, A., Rezvy, G., Hansen, V. and Olstad, R. (2006) The effect of gender in diagnosing early schizophrenia. *Social Psychiatry and Psychiatric Epidemiology*, 41 (7): 549.

Longenecker, J., Genderson, J., Dickinson, D., Malley, J., Elvevåg, B., Weinberger, D.R. and Gold, J. (2010) Where have all the women gone? Participant gender in epidemiological and non-epidemiological research of schizophrenia. *Schizophrenia Research*, 119 (1–3): 240–245.

Whaley, A.L. (2004) A two-stage method for the study of cultural bias in the diagnosis of schizophrenia in African Americans. *Journal of Black Psychology*, 30 (2): 167–186.

World Health Organization (WHO) (2018) *International Classification of Diseases, 11th revision (ICD-11)*. Geneva, Switzerland: World Health Organization.

Chapter 3
Biological explanations for schizophrenia

Spec check

Biological explanations for schizophrenia: genetics, the dopamine hypothesis and neural correlates.

AO1 (Knowledge and understanding): What are the biological explanations for schizophrenia?

How does biology influence mental health?

Mental disorders are generally regarded to be different from physical disorders in that they are problems with the way a person's mind is working.

According to the World Health Organisation:

> Mental disorders comprise a broad range of problems, with different symptoms. However, they are generally characterized by some combination of abnormal thoughts, emotions, behaviour and relationships with others.
>
> (www.who.int/mental_health/management/en/)

This definition seems to place mental disorders in the area of the mind and behaviour as it mentions thoughts, feelings and relationships with others, however, it is questionable whether we can separate our minds from our physical bodies and, in particular, from our brains. This is part of a long-standing debate in psychology concerning whether we can separate our mind and body or whether they are the same thing. Biological psychologists are confident in arguing that the mind is ultimately just another part of the brain and therefore we can locate the cause of all mental disorders in the brain and the body.

This is important to our attempt to understand the biological explanations for schizophrenia because it helps us to understand the arguments made about the causes of mental disorders put forward by these biological psychologists. These arguments can essentially be divided into three types:

- Genetic explanations relating to how inherited genes affect behaviour.
- Neurochemical explanations relating to the workings of the nervous system.
- Neurological explanations relating to the structure and function of the brain.

However, it may be possible to argue that genes are behind all of these – that they affect the working of the nervous system and the structure of the brain, so, in the end, everything is genetic!

> **Think!**
>
> Are the mind and the brain the same thing? If not, what is the mind?
>
> Is everything caused by your genes? What problems are there with this explanation?
>
> Why is it useful to explain all mental disorders in terms of physical malfunction?

Genetics and schizophrenia

In its simplest form the genetic explanation suggests that schizophrenia is inherited and therefore the more closely related you are to someone with schizophrenia, then the more likely you are to suffer with it. Evidence for the link between family-relatedness and schizophrenia has been tested many times and an influential study by Gottesman in 1991 showed how closely family-relatedness was linked to schizophrenia.

This simple explanation should be easy to test. We could study people with schizophrenia and test their close relatives. If we found that those relatives were more likely to suffer with the disorder than people who were unrelated, then we could show that schizophrenia was genetic. However, it clearly isn't that simple because we cannot identify whether the disorder came about due to the genetic link or due to the fact of living with someone with schizophrenia. This would also explain how being more closely related would lead to a higher incidence of schizophrenia, because the more time you spend with them, the more likely you are to pick up their behaviour.

Candidate genes

This more sophisticated version of the genetic argument has come about due to the fact that we no longer have to simply rely on family Studies, adoption studies and twin studies, as we now have the ability to use gene mapping to identify candidate genes, which show which genes make someone more susceptible to developing schizophrenia. A number of studies have examined specific genes and have been able to suggest that there are specific schizophrenia susceptibility genes. However, Ripke et al. (2014) were able to bring together data from genome-wide studies, covering nearly 37,000 cases of schizophrenia, from which they were able to identify 128 genetic associations with schizophrenia, of which 83 had not been identified before. The importance of this is that many of these associations were related to the role of neurotransmitters and tie in well with the treatments associated with biological explanations.

Question time

What kinds of treatments are associated with biological explanations?

Are there any other possible treatments that could be used to treat genetic disorders?

Are there any problems with biological treatments?

The dopamine hypothesis

Neurotransmitters are the chemical messengers of the brain, serving to transmit messages through the nervous system at the synapse. One of the most significant neurotransmitters identified in the biological explanation of schizophrenia is dopamine, which is a neurotransmitter that plays a role in pleasure, motivation, learning, movement and emotional responses. Stimulants increase the levels of dopamine in the brain and help to give us some idea of how dopamine might affect our behaviour.

The effects of increased levels of dopamine lie at the heart of the first version of the dopamine hypothesis, as it was discovered that medication used to treat schizophrenia lowers dopamine activity and that drugs that produce schizophrenia-like symptoms, such as amphetamines, increase dopamine activity. These findings led Snyder (1976) to argue that increased levels of dopamine can lead to the onset of schizophrenia.

This first version of the hypothesis was later modified by Davis et al. (1991) following the discovery that not all patients with schizophrenia had increased dopamine activity. Version two of the hypothesis brought in a new more sophisticated argument that recognised there was an issue with the simple notion of an excess of dopamine leading to schizophrenia and argued that dopamine abnormalities vary according to the region of the brain in which they occur. The conclusion was that hyperdopaminergia (high levels of dopamine) in the subcortex, the central parts of the brain containing the mesolimbic dopamine pathway, was responsible for mainly positive symptoms, but that hypodopaminergia (low levels of dopamine) in the prefrontal cortex containing the mesocortical dopamine pathway, was responsible for mainly negative symptoms.

A third version, referred to as the 'final common pathway' by Howes and Kapur (2009), argued that 'multiple hits' interact to result in the abnormal regulation of dopamine. These multiple hits combine genes, brain dysfunction, stress and drug intake, as well as environmental factors such as urban living, which all work together to bring about abnormal dopamine activity. Furthermore, Howes and Kapur argued that problems in dopamine regulation occurred at the pre-synaptic level and, therefore, drugs used to block dopamine reception could make dopamine abnormalities worse.

This all suggests that dopamine does play a role in the experience of schizophrenia, but it may be too simplistic to only deal with the effect of increased levels of dopamine once all of this has already occurred, and, therefore, a more sophisticated approach to treatment is required.

The neural correlates of schizophrenia

The study of neural correlates of schizophrenia is based on the idea that specific abnormalities in the brain may be so closely related to the symptoms of schizophrenia that we could argue that it is these abnormalities that are responsible for the development of schizophrenia.

In the past, potential brain abnormalities in people with schizophrenia would have been studied using post-mortem examinations on dead schizophrenics. However, modern scanning techniques such as fMRI have made it possible to identify areas of the brain that are either damaged or not functioning normally, and these studies have been further enhanced by the use of diffusion tensor imaging (DTI), which mainly assesses changes in white matter.

Rotarska-Jagiela et al. (2009) used DTI to assess the white matter activity of a group of paranoid schizophrenic patients with a history of auditory hallucinations and then compared that with the white matter activity of a group of healthy controls. They found reduced connectivity in the white matter of certain areas of the brains of the schizophrenic patients but, importantly, also found increased connectivity in their arcuate fasciculus, which is a region of the brain known to play a role in language processing. Their findings indicated that the disturbance in this area of the brain was correlated with increased severity of auditory hallucinations.

Neural imaging using fMRI has also been used to measure the relationship between brain activity and negative symptoms, with a particular focus on the ventral striatum, which is associated with decision-making and reward-related behaviour. The anticipation of rewards is related to motivation and, as such, is regarded as important in avolition; and the receipt of rewards is related to the pleasurable effect of rewards and, as such, is regarded as important in depression. A disturbance in the ventral striatum in people with schizophrenia could indicate a relationship between this area of the brain and the development of the negative symptoms of schizophrenia. Simon et al. (2010) used fMRI scans with a group of 15 patients with schizophrenia and compared them with a group of 15 healthy controls. They found that there were no significant differences in general neural activity between the two groups when undertaking a task that involved both the anticipation and receipt of rewards. However, they did find that ventral-striatal activation was negatively correlated with apathy during reward anticipation and that ventral-striatal activation was also negatively correlated with depression during reward receipt. This indicates that reduced activity in this area of the brain is a neural correlate of avolition and depression.

Question time

What do these studies tell us about schizophrenia?
Can we conclude from this that it is biological factors alone that are responsible for the development of schizophrenia? Why? Or why not?

Mini plenary

Without referring back to the text, provide definitions of the following terms:

Candidate genes _____

Hyperdopaminergia _____

Neural correlates _____

AO2 (Application of knowledge): How does this apply in practice?

Interleave me now

Methodological issues

One of the important considerations when looking at the application of explanations in psychology to the real world is what methods have been used. The choice of method is most likely to be related to the needs of any particular study, but it may also be related to the need to be able to show that the findings of the study can be applied beyond the situation in which they have been studied. There is a range of methods referred to above and each of these will be considered in relation to its ability to be applied to the 'real' world.

Methods used in biological explanations: family studies, adoption studies, twin studies, post-mortem examinations, fMRI studies

The use of these methods is outlined in Table 3.1, with the strengths and weaknesses identified. The spaces in the Application column indicate prompts to write down your comments with regard to the potential application of these studies to real life. (The first one has been done for you.)

Table 3.1 Methods used in biological explanations

Method	Description	Strength	Weakness	Application
Family studies	Studies that look into the percentage likelihood of a person inheriting schizophrenia from a blood relative.	Family members share a predictable proportion of genes so are easier to control.	Difficult to rule out the influence of the environment on behaviour as relatives often live together.	Can be used to show if a range of behaviours run in families, e.g. IQ, aggression and mental disorders such as schizophrenia.

Table 3.1 continued

Method	Description	Strength	Weakness	Application
Adoption studies	Studies that compare the percentage likelihood of developing schizophrenia for those adopted out of an environment with schizophrenic parents.	Makes it easier to rule out the influence of the environment as people are living in a different environment to their parents.	Children are often placed in homes that are similar to those they have left, making it harder to identify a real difference.	
Twin studies	Studies that investigate the percentage likelihood of developing schizophrenia if a person has a twin with the disorder.	Identical twins are virtually genetically identical making it possible to show a clear genetic link.	Identical twins are sometimes treated identically, meaning that it may be the environment that affects their similar behaviour.	
Post-mortem examinations	Medical examinations of human bodies conducted after the person has died.	Provides a hands-on approach that is impossible with a living brain.	Causation may be difficult to establish as it could be that any observed damage could have been caused by the disorder rather than the cause.	
fMRI studies	A brain scan that measures brain activity by detecting changes associated with blood flow when someone is doing a task.	Provides clear and detailed images with less risk of harm than other forms of scan.	Reliant on the patient being still during the procedure.	

Think!

Is there anything that these types of studies have in common?

Are they all equally useful, depending on the needs of the specific study?

Does this suggest that such methods can be applied successfully to the real world? Why? Or why not?

Interleave me now

The nature–nurture debate

This is one of the oldest debates in psychology and considers the extent to which psychological processes can be put down to innate or environmental factors. If they can be seen to be present from birth, and therefore innate, then we can argue that nature is the most dominant factor. However, if they can be shown to have developed during the life cycle, then we can argue that nurture is the most dominant factor. Naturally, this rather simplistic distinction fails to take into account a number of mediating factors that come into play in the consideration of each. For example, we may inherit a predisposition that is not obvious at birth but comes into play later in life. It may or may not be related to specific life events that have occurred, but it could be said to have been influential in the particular psychological process or behaviour that we are studying.

Nature–nurture and schizophrenia

Biological explanations for schizophrenia bring the nature–nurture debate into sharp focus. We are bound to need to consider the extent to which the development of schizophrenia is influenced by natural, biological factors, which would have developed regardless of any environmental factors, and compare these to the extent to which schizophrenia is influenced by life events, which combine to make someone vulnerable to developing schizophrenia.

The nature side

The biological factors above might all be related to genes and, if so, this provides considerable support for the nature side of the debate. Findings from studies such as those outlined above from Ripke et al. have suggested that there may be multiple genes involved and therefore schizophrenia may be polygenic, meaning it requires a number of genes working together to put a person at risk. On the one hand, this could provide support for the nature argument, as it supports the idea that some people are born at greater risk of developing schizophrenia than others. However, on the other hand, it may not provide much support because it fails to show the 'smoking gun', that could be seen to be the cause of schizophrenia. With so many factors involved – remember Ripke identified 128 genetic associations – it is hard to say that there is a gene for schizophrenia; therefore genes become one factor among many that could be seen to be responsible for the development of schizophrenia.

The nurture side

The psychological explanations outlined in Chapter 4 of this book provide arguments and analysis suggesting that biological explanations alone cannot account for the development of schizophrenia, and it may be that psychological/environmental factors play a bigger role. One environmental factor that has gained significant interest in recent years has been the relationship between childhood trauma and schizophrenia. Some studies have suggested that children who experience severe trauma are three times more likely to develop schizophrenia. Furthermore, some studies have gone on to suggest that certain symptoms of schizophrenia are associated with specific forms of trauma. Bentall et al. (2012) found that hallucinations were more closely associated with childhood sexual abuse, while paranoia was associated with being raised in a children's home. These findings provide evidence for the nurture side but still don't provide a causal explanation as, just like the genetic explanations, they are simply able to identify risk factors, rather than any kind of definitive evidence that will settle the argument once and for all.

Question time

What does this tell us about the nature–nurture debate?

What do you think? Is schizophrenia more closely related to the nature side or the nurture side?

How could we combine nature and nurture to provide a more complete explanation?

Mini plenary

Studies have shown a relationship between early childhood trauma and the development of the positive symptoms of schizophrenia, particularly hallucinations. However, no such link has been found for the negative symptoms such as avolition.

Explain these findings with reference to the influence of both nature and nurture on schizophrenia?

AO3 (Analysis and evaluation of knowledge): How useful is this explanation?

Why is there a problem with causation in biological explanations?

The problem of showing cause and effect in correlational studies is well established. It is difficult to show that one variable causes another when the many other variables that could have an impact are neither controlled nor measured. Consequently, all that we can ever hope to do is to show that there is a significant relationship between the two variables, suggesting that these variables may be more significant than other variables (although we can't even be sure of that if we haven't measured them).

This problem is particularly relevant to the neural correlates explanation of schizophrenia. Although we may be able to establish that there is a relationship between the negative symptoms of schizophrenia and reduced activity in the ventral striatum, as Simon et al. (2010) did, we cannot be certain that the lack of activity caused the symptoms of depression or whether the feelings of depression caused the reduced activity.

Similarly, in genetic studies, which look at the relationship between family-relatedness and the increased likelihood of developing schizophrenia, we cannot be certain that it was shared genes that caused the symptoms of schizophrenia. It may be that sharing an environment with someone who has schizophrenia makes a person more likely to develop the disorder. There are too many uncontrolled, unmeasured variables to make that assumption. However, we can say that family-relatedness is associated with schizophrenia.

Finally, it seems that there is strong evidence to show a relationship between schizophrenia and dopamine levels, such that increased levels of dopamine are associated with the development of schizophrenia. However, it is much harder to establish if these increased levels are the cause of schizophrenia or are, in fact, caused by having schizophrenia. It could be that having severe schizophrenic symptoms causes the levels of dopamine in these individuals to rise and, unless we are able to study people before they develop schizophrenia, it will remain virtually impossible to establish the cause. Even then, as noted by Howes and Kapur (2009), there are multiple hits that are likely to be responsible, so just artificially raising dopamine levels would probably be unlikely to have the effect expected.

This suggests that most of the biological methods used to show the link between biological factors and schizophrenia are unlikely to show us the complete cause of schizophrenia, which has significant implications for the treatment of the disorder in both the short and long term.

> **Think!**
>
> What do you think the implications for treatment would be if the methods used don't show us the complete cause of schizophrenia? In the long-term? In the short-term?

What are the implications for treatment if we accept these biological explanations?

As stated at the start of this chapter, part of the appeal of biological explanations is that if we can identify a biological cause, then we may be able to provide a biological treatment to deal with it, which would have a range of practical benefits. Unfortunately, nothing is quite as simple as that and an examination of the different types of explanations may well indicate the difficulty of developing drug treatments that would deal with all of them.

The most obvious candidate for the use of drug treatment would be the dopamine hypothesis. It seems logical that if we are able to isolate dopamine as the cause, or at least a significant factor, in the development of schizophrenia, then we should be able to develop drugs that deal with that by blocking dopamine receptors. To some extent this is true as it has been one of the main uses of antipsychotic medication over the last few decades. However, as Howes and Kapur (2009) have shown, if the issue is occurring at the pre-synaptic level then blocking dopamine receptors may be ineffective as they are targeting the wrong area.

Ripke et al. (2014) showed that most of the genetic variations identified in their study were ones that affected dopamine levels and, from that point of view, it would seem logical to expect that using antipsychotic drugs to target dopamine receptors would be effective. However, they also noted that the results of their studies have identified that schizophrenia is polygenic and some studies, e.g. Zhang et al. (2019), have shown that patients with a high polygenic risk of developing schizophrenia are less likely to respond to antipsychotic medication.

This suggests that although biological explanations provide a strong theoretical basis for the development of antipsychotic medication, particularly those that target dopamine, it is unlikely to be as simple as that in practice. However, such antipsychotic medication does remain at the forefront of the treatment of schizophrenia and is likely to remain so until something better comes along.

What environmental factors influence schizophrenia?

Although this chapter has been devoted to outlining the biological explanations for schizophrenia, there have still been a few references to environmental factors that are linked to schizophrenia. One of the more prominent among these has been the suggestion that childhood trauma might be linked to the disorder. Studies have looked at physical abuse, sexual abuse, parental neglect, maternal deprivation, death of a parent, bullying, spending time in a children's home, and a range of other factors linked to childhood trauma.

Bentall et al. (2012) found that not only was childhood trauma linked to the development of schizophrenia, but that specific symptoms of schizophrenia could be shown to be linked to specific forms of trauma. For example, hallucinations were linked to sexual abuse and paranoia was linked to spending time in a children's home.

However, with such a wide range of studies, each showing different factors related to the development of schizophrenia, it has been difficult to show that there is sufficient evidence to show an overall connection between childhood trauma and the disorder.

Varese et al. (2012) attempted to overcome this problem by using a meta-analysis of over 40 studies that had all looked at the effect of childhood trauma (defined as sexual abuse, physical abuse, emotional/psychological abuse, neglect, parental death, and bullying) on the prevalence of psychosis. They found that there was a significant association between childhood trauma and psychosis for all of the types of trauma studied, and that there was no evidence that any one type of trauma was a stronger predictor of psychosis than another.

While this does seem to show that childhood trauma is a major factor in the development of psychosis, it doesn't rule out other factors and it still leaves the question of causation unanswered. As the studies were for psychosis as a general category, rather than simply for schizophrenia, we may still have a problem in identifying a specific explanation for schizophrenia. However, recent developments discussed in

Chapter 2 might suggest that it is extremely difficult to identify schizophrenia as a single disorder anyway.

> **Think!**
>
> What recent developments from Chapter 2 might change our view of what schizophrenia is?

What are the ethical implications of identifying biological factors as the cause of schizophrenia?

Ethical implications are concerned with the wider and long-term impacts of research and theory. We need to consider the effect of providing explanations based on factors that could have an effect on the wider community. Biological explanations can have both positive and negative impacts upon those identified as suffering with mental health problems, and these can be particularly problematic for those suffering with schizophrenia due to the perception of the disorder as being dangerous and in need of a solution.

The potential ethical problems involved in labelling and stigmatising those with mental illness, and with schizophrenia in particular, as being 'weird' or 'odd' and 'not like everyone else' have led to a deliberate approach of trying to get the public to see people with a mental illness as being ill in the same way as those with a physical illness are ill. This approach therefore emphasises the genetic and neural explanations for that illness and attempts to break down the prejudice and discrimination that can sometimes be aimed at those with mental illness, which is a particular problem for those with schizophrenia.

However, there is some evidence that the approach has not only been unsuccessful, but it also may have led to increased fear and prejudice towards those with schizophrenia. Read et al. (2006) found evidence for this effect in their research into the effectiveness of the campaign to have mental illness recognised as a genetic or neural illness. In a review of a large number of studies from across the world, they found that efforts to change the public perception of mental illness to one that emphasised genetic and neural factors had actually resulted in increased fear and desire for social distance due to an increased perception of unpredictability on the part of those with mental illness, and that this was particularly true for those with schizophrenia. However, it seems that campaigns of this sort are continuing, which can be seen from similar, recent campaigns in the UK to have mental illness thought of as being like any other illness.

It seems that biological explanations intended to make the general public feel more at ease with those with mental illness, on the basis that it could happen to any one of us, just like any other illness, have not entirely had the desired outcome. In many of the studies reviewed, it seemed that making people understand that those with mental illness weren't responsible for their disorder, caused people to fear that the mentally ill might be out of control and potentially violent. This was not, of course, the intended outcome, but unfortunately sometimes research and theory can have unexpected outcomes that may require a more socially sensitive approach to be taken.

Question time

What are the alternatives to the biological explanations outlined in this chapter?

Are these alternatives likely to be enough on their own to explain schizophrenia?

Are these alternatives better or worse than biological explanations? Can they be seen as complementary?

Mini plenary

Using the evaluation points above, try to identify arguments for and against biological explanations for schizophrenia.

Arguments for	Arguments against

A modern issue: does cannabis cause schizophrenia?

The connection between schizophrenia and cannabis use continues to be a source of debate, although not always in the way expected. There is a growing understanding that the two are connected in some way, but the actual connection isn't always clear, i.e. whether cannabis causes genetically vulnerable individuals to develop schizophrenia, or whether people with a genetic vulnerability to schizophrenia are just more likely to use cannabis.

New research

Cannabis use 'genetically linked' to schizophrenia

Hiemstra et al. (2018)

This study aimed to identify whether the reported connection between schizophrenia and substance use might be explained by a genetic vulnerability to schizophrenia.

In order to find this out they conducted a longitudinal study of 372 young people initially aged 13–16 and then again at the ages of 16–20. They compared their polygenic risk scores for schizophrenia with any associated increase of substance use over the years of the study.

They found that a higher genetic vulnerability to schizophrenia was associated with a significant increase in cannabis use at the ages of 16–20. However, there was no such association for smoking and alcohol.

This suggests that the connection between cannabis use and schizophrenia may be related to genetic factors, because those with an increased genetic predisposition to schizophrenia were more likely to use cannabis and to use it in larger quantities than those without the genes. However, they did also find a not quite significant association suggesting the complete opposite, so the findings are not 100% conclusive.

Question time

What does this article tell us about cannabis use and schizophrenia?

What does it tell us about genes and schizophrenia?

Why might the connection between genetic vulnerability and cannabis use not be 100% conclusive?

What other factors might push someone towards cannabis use?

Chapter plenary

1. How does biology influence mental health?
2. What are the three types of biological explanations for schizophrenia?
3. What are candidate genes in relation to the genetic view of schizophrenia?
4. What is the dopamine hypothesis in relation to schizophrenia?
5. What is meant by the neural correlates of schizophrenia?
6. What are the methods used to study biological explanations for schizophrenia?
7. What are the strengths and weaknesses of these methods?
8. How does the nature–nurture debate apply to explanations for schizophrenia?
9. Why is there a problem with causation in relation to biological explanations for schizophrenia?
10. What environmental factors influence schizophrenia?
11. What are the implications for treatment if we accept biological explanations for schizophrenia?
12. What are the ethical implications of identifying biological factors as the cause of schizophrenia?
13. Does cannabis cause schizophrenia?

Glossary

Key word	Definition
Adoption studies	Studies that compare the percentage likelihood of developing schizophrenia for those adopted out of an environment with schizophrenic parents.
Arcuate fasciculus	The arcuate fasciculus is a white matter bundle that connects the frontal, parietal, and temporal lobes. The arcuate plays a key role in the left hemisphere in language processing.
Avolition	The inability to engage in activity that might result in them achieving some desired goal.
Candidate genes	Specific genes that may be responsible for the development of schizophrenia.
Depression	A condition that causes negative feelings and loss of interest in activities previously enjoyed.
Diffusion tensor imaging (DTI)	A technique that uses an MRI scanner to identify the linkages and structure of white matter in the brain.
Family studies	Studies that look into the percentage likelihood of someone inheriting schizophrenia from a blood relative.
fMRI	Stands for functional magnetic resonance imaging and measures brain activity by detecting changes associated with blood flow.
Genome-wide studies	Studies that use gene mapping to identify genetic variations in a particular population.
Hyperdopaminergia	A condition of having too much dopamine.
Hypodopaminergia	A condition of having too little dopamine.
Mesocortical dopamine pathway	One of the four major dopamine pathways in the brain; it is connected to the prefrontal cortex area of the brain.
Mesolimbic dopamine pathway	One of the four major dopamine pathways in the brain; it is in the central area of the brain.
Polygenic	The idea that schizophrenia may be influenced by two or more genes.
Post-mortem examinations	Medical examinations of human bodies conducted after the person has died.
Smoking gun	An analogy with finding a shooter with a smoking gun in their hand, it has come to mean evidence that cannot be argued against.

Key word	Definition
Twin studies	Studies that investigate the percentage likelihood of developing schizophrenia if a person has a twin with the disorder.
Ventral striatum	Part of the brain associated with decision-making and reward-related behaviour.
White matter	One of the components of the brain, it is responsible for transmitting signals from one part of the brain to another.

Plenary: Exam-style questions and answers with advisory comments

Question 1.

Explain the role of genes in the development of schizophrenia   [4 marks]

Marks for this question: AO1 = 4

Advice: In a question like this, it's important to make sure you are clearly explaining their role, rather than just identifying/outlining what they are. This question might be difficult as it is easy to fall into the trap of being repetitive, so you need to make sure your explanation is making clearly different points. There is no need to provide any analysis or evaluation as all of the marks are for AO1: Knowledge and understanding.

Possible answer: The genetic explanation suggests that schizophrenia is inherited and therefore the more closely related you are to someone with schizophrenia, then the more likely you are to suffer with it. This explanation has come about due to the use of family, twin and adoption studies but more recently researchers have been able to use gene mapping to identify candidate genes, which are genes that may make someone particularly susceptible to schizophrenia. These recent developments have led to an understanding that schizophrenia may be polygenic and therefore caused by two or more genes. These findings suggest that the role of genetics in schizophrenia may be a lot more complicated than a simple matter of inheriting a single gene and that it may require multiple genes working alongside other biological and environmental factors for schizophrenia to develop.

Question 2.

Describe and evaluate biological explanations for schizophrenia. [16 marks]

Marks for this question: AO1 = 6 and AO3 = 10

Advice: This question is looking for both skills of knowledge and understanding and analysis and evaluation. As there are 6 marks for AO1 and 10 for AO3, there should be greater emphasis on the evaluation. However, all such extended writing questions are marked holistically and therefore it is important that the knowledge is accurate and detailed and that the evaluation is clear and effective.

Possible answer: Biological explanations for schizophrenia focus on three possible factors that may be responsible for the development of schizophrenia: genetics; the dopamine hypothesis, suggesting that excess levels of the neurotransmitter are responsible; and neural correlates, specifically related to the structure and function of the brain. In this answer, I will focus on just two of those factors, the dopamine hypothesis and neurological issues.

Dopamine is a neurotransmitter that is associated with pleasure and motivation and is increased by stimulants, which may provide a clue as to its role in behaviour. In 1976 Snyder put forward the hypothesis that increased levels of dopamine in the brain are related to the development of schizophrenia. This was discovered after it was found that stimulant drugs such as amphetamines produce schizophrenia-like behaviour and that the drugs used to treat schizophrenia decrease the levels of dopamine in the brain.

In 1991, Davis introduced a new, more sophisticated version of the hypothesis, after it was noticed that not all patients with schizophrenia had high levels of dopamine. This second version argued that hyperdopaminergia (increased levels of dopamine) in the subcortex was related to the positive symptoms of schizophrenia, but that hypodopaminergia (decreased levels) in the prefrontal cortex was related to the negative symptoms. More recently, Howes and Kapur have introduced a third version of the hypothesis, suggesting that 'multiple hits' are required from a range of sources, including genes, the environment and levels of dopamine, to bring on schizophrenia.

Neural correlates have been identified as a possible source for schizophrenia, as it has been found that abnormalities in the structure and function of the brain are so closely related to the development of schizophrenia, that they must play a role. Advances in technology, specifically the use of fMRI and diffusion tensor imaging (DTI) have allowed these areas to be identified. Simon et al. looked at the role of the ventral stratum, which is an area of the brain known to play a role in the anticipation and receipt of rewards. Using fMRI scans they were able to show that underactivity in this part of the brain was associated with both avolition and depression, suggesting that it may be this part that is a neural correlate for schizophrenia. In a similar way, Rotarska-Jagiela et al. have been able to use DTI to show how increases in the activity of white matter in the arcuate fasciculus (an area of the brain known to play a role in language) is associated with auditory hallucinations.

Support for the role of biological factors has come from recent findings suggesting that schizophrenia may be linked with the use of cannabis, as this suggests that the introduction of this chemical into the brain of a person who is susceptible to schizophrenia may be enough to bring on psychosis. Research by Hiemstra et al. has found a link between a genetic predisposition for schizophrenia and the use of cannabis. However, their findings seemed to indicate that, rather than cannabis bringing about the schizophrenia, it was actually the other way round and that having the gene for schizophrenia was more likely to push a person towards cannabis use.

This problem of causation is a continuing one for all of the biological explanations, as it is hard to establish whether increased, or indeed decreased, levels of dopamine in areas of the brain are the cause of schizophrenia or whether the schizophrenia is the cause of the changed levels. Similarly, it is hard to establish whether the decreased activity in areas of the brain studied by Simon et al. is the cause of symptoms such as avolition and depression or whether having these symptoms is the cause of the decreased activity.

Although some of these findings provide support for the biological explanations, they ignore the role of environmental factors and as such could be accused of being biologically reductionist. In recent years, there has been a growing acceptance that childhood trauma is related to schizophrenia. Bentall et al. found that not only was childhood trauma linked to the development of schizophrenia, but that specific symptoms of schizophrenia could be shown to be linked to specific forms of trauma, such that hallucinations were linked to sexual abuse and paranoia was linked to spending time in a children's home. These factors could be just as influential in the development of schizophrenia as any biological processes and could in fact be responsible for the biological changes that have then been identified as linked to schizophrenia in later studies. This is a problem for the study of schizophrenia as it's ethically unacceptable to experiment on the effects of these changes so it's only ever possible to study someone with schizophrenia once they have already had it for some time, consequently cause and effect is difficult to establish.

Other ethical implications arising from any attempt to use biological processes to explain schizophrenia come from research by Read et al., who found that attempts by governments and the medical profession to promote the idea that mental illness is an illness just like any other, may have been well-intentioned but have actually had the reverse effect of causing further prejudice. The use of the campaign was an attempt to normalise mental illness by suggesting that it could affect anyone just like physical illnesses. However, Read et al. found that it added to the belief that mental illnesses, particularly schizophrenia, were out of people's control and therefore more dangerous, increasing the fear of the general public towards people with schizophrenia.

The biological approach has contributed to the treatment of schizophrenia, however, as the most common treatment is antipsychotic medication and, as levels of dopamine have been well established as having a strong correlation with the disorder, it has seemed sensible to use drugs that alter these levels to treat it. However, it isn't always that simple and Zhang et al. found that those with a high polygenic risk of developing schizophrenia were actually less likely to respond to antipsychotic medication. This suggests that we may need a more sophisticated approach to the treatment of schizophrenia. This is likely to come from explanations that include nature and nurture as factors and propose treatments that use a combination of biological and psychological approaches.

References

Bentall, R.P., Wickham, S., Shevlin, M. and Varese, F. (2012) Do specific early-life adversities lead to specific symptoms of psychosis? A study from the 2007 Adult Psychiatric Morbidity Survey. *Schizophrenia Bulletin*, 38 (4): 734–740.

Davis, K.L., Kahn, R.S., Ko, G. and Davidson, M. (1991) Dopamine in schizophrenia: A review and reconceptualization. *The American Journal of Psychiatry*, 148 (11): 1474.

Gottesman, I.I. (1991) *Schizophrenia Genesis: The Origins of Madness.* New York: W.H. Freeman.

Hiemstra, M., Nelemans, S.A., Branje, S., Van Eijk, K.R., Hottenga, J.J., Vinkers, C.H., Van Lier, P., Meeus, W. and Boks, M.P. (2018) Genetic vulnerability to schizophrenia is associated with cannabis use patterns during adolescence. *Drug and Alcohol Dependence*, 190: 143–150.

Howes, O.D. and Kapur, S. (2009) The dopamine hypothesis of schizophrenia: Version III—The final common pathway. *Schizophrenia Bulletin*, 35 (3): 549–562.

Power, R.A., Verweij, K.J., Zuhair, M., Montgomery, G.W., Henders, A.K., Madden, P.A., Medland, S.E., Wray, N.R. et al. (2014) Genetic predisposition to schizophrenia associated with increased use of cannabis. *Molecular Psychiatry*, 19: 1201–1204.

Read, J., Haslam, N., Sayce, L. and Davies, E. (2006) Prejudice and schizophrenia: A review of the 'mental illness is an illness like any other' approach. *Acta Psychiatrica Scandinavica*, 114 (5): 303–318.

Ripke, S., Neale, B.M., Corvin, A., Walters, J.T., Farh, K.H., Holmans, P.A., Lee, P., Bulik-Sullivan, B., Collier, D.A., Huang, H. and Pers, T.H. (2014) Biological insights from 108 schizophrenia-associated genetic loci. *Nature*, 511 (7510): 421.

Rotarska-Jagiela, A., Oertel-Knoechel, V., DeMartino, F., van de Ven, V., Formisano, E., Roebroeck, A., Rami, A., Schoenmeyer, R. (2009) Anatomical brain connectivity and positive symptoms of schizophrenia: A diffusion tensor imaging study. *Psychiatry Research: Neuroimaging*, 174 (1): 9–16.

Simon, J.J., Biller, A., Walther, S., Roesch-Ely, D., Stippich, C., Weisbrod, M. and Kaiser, S. (2010) Neural correlates of reward processing in schizophrenia – Relationship to apathy and depression. *Schizophrenia Research*, 118 (1–3): 154–161.

Snyder, S.H., (1976) The dopamine hypothesis of schizophrenia: Focus on the dopamine receptor. *The American Journal of Psychiatry*, 133 (2): 197–202.

Varese, F., Smeets, F., Drukker, M., Lieverse, R., Lataster, T., Viechtbauer, W., Read, J., van Os, J. and Bentall, R.P. (2012) Childhood adversities increase the risk of psychosis: A meta-analysis of patient-control, prospective- and cross-sectional cohort studies. *Schizophrenia Bulletin*, 38 (4): 661–671.

Zhang, J.P., Robinson, D., Yu, J., Gallego, J., Fleischhacker, W.W., Kahn, R.S., Crespo-Facorro, B., Vasquez-Bourgon, J., Kane, J.M., Malhotra, K.A. and Lencz, T. (2019) Schizophrenia polygenic risk score as a predictor of antipsychotic efficacy in first-episode psychosis. *American Journal of Psychiatry*, 176 (1): 21–28.

Chapter 4
Psychological explanations for schizophrenia

Spec check

Psychological explanations for schizophrenia: family dysfunction and cognitive explanations, including dysfunctional thought processing.

AO1 (Knowledge and understanding): What are the psychological explanations for schizophrenia?

Psychological influences on mental health

In Chapter 3, the World Health Organisation (WHO) definition for mental disorders suggested a clear role for the mind and behaviour, rather than for biological factors. These psychological factors include a variety of influences, ranging from specific environmental factors that have a social influence on us and alter our behaviour to factors that are directly related to mental processes and affect our understanding of the world around us. All these factors can affect our normal daily lives through their influence on our thoughts and feelings, which may sometimes be adaptive but at times can be maladaptive too.

Psychological influences focus on the factors that have caused a person's mind and behaviour to develop in the way that it has, rather than the biological influences on their brain and nervous system looked at in Chapter 3. These psychological influences are likely to be those that relate to a person's upbringing and their treatment by those around them, e.g. by their parents. In the past, psychologists have gone as far as to blame the mother for the way that she has brought up her children, specifically with the notion of the schizophrenogenic mother and the suggestion that cold, rejecting mothers who try to have too much control over their children's lives are the cause of schizophrenia. Fortunately, such theories are less common today as we develop a greater understanding of the range of factors that affect our mental health.

In the Psychopathology section of Paper 1, you will have looked at cognitive explanations for mental disorders and the possibility that the way that a person's mind attempts to make sense of incoming sensory information could be the cause of disorders such as depression. This explanation can apply to other mental disorders too, and any attempt to explain the psychological influences on schizophrenia will inevitably need to look at the possibility that faulty mental processing has a part to play in the development of schizophrenia.

> **Think!**
>
> Is parental treatment likely to be an important factor in a person's mental health?
>
> Why doesn't a person always make good sense of the information coming into their mind?
>
> Why might psychological factors be better than biological factors in explaining the cause of schizophrenia?

Family dysfunction and schizophrenia

One definition of the family is a group, consisting of two parents and their children living together as a unit. In this sense it suggests that the family is a highly functional unit that serves a useful purpose and often, of course, it is serving a very useful purpose in providing security and comfort for those in it. However, this isn't always the case, as is suggested in the title of this section – sometimes families can be dysfunctional and, far from providing security and comfort, can lead to insecurity and discomfort.

Family dysfunction explanations for schizophrenia can be broken down into two parts: those that focus on family communication as a risk factor in the development of schizophrenia symptoms and those that focus on family communication as a factor in the relapse of those suffering from schizophrenia when they return to the family home.

Double bind theory

This theory suggests that the problem is caused by parents using social interactions that place the child in a 'no win' situation. Bateson et al. (1956) put forward the double bind theory. They suggest that the family interactions are contradictory in that the parents are giving their children mixed messages that leave the young person confused about how to react. The behaviour of the parent is likely to have (at least) two sides to it; one involves the parent behaving in a hostile manner to the child and the other involves the parent trying to make up for their hostile behaviour by (simulating) loving behaviour. If the child were to respond to this simulated behaviour, it would result in further hostile behaviour; but if they don't respond to it, then the child is likely to be punished (with hostility). This is the double bind that Bateson et al. are referring to: the child simply cannot win, no matter what they do. This situation causes confusion, which can lead to paranoia and the possibility of delusional behaviour as the child has to cope with the conflicting demands of the parent. The child may also withdraw into a world of their own, leading to a flat affect in order to avoid having to show any emotional response to these double bind situations.

Bateson et al. aren't suggesting that this is the only factor in the development of schizophrenia, nor are they suggesting that it is the only form of communication that occurs. What they are suggesting is that it would have had to have happened regularly to have this kind of effect and that it places the child at risk of developing schizophrenic symptoms. Furthermore, they do not suggest that this kind of behaviour is purely the domain of the mother but that either parent could behave in this way. As for the other parent, Bateson et al. consider that the other parent may not be strong enough to prevent this kind of behaviour, or they may, more likely, be providing the contradictory messages that are causing the problem, further leading to the confused and paranoid behaviour displayed by the child.

Expressed emotion (EE)

Another factor in communication style that has been shown to affect patients with schizophrenia who have returned to the family home is the level of expressed emotion that they are greeted with on their return. Expressed emotion is concerned with the level of criticism and hostility directed towards the patient by family members, combined with emotional over-involvement in the life of the patient. For example, the family might express concern about even the most minor matters in the patient's life, such as setting their alarm clock. It has been suggested that a high level of expressed emotion is associated with a relapse into schizophrenic symptoms in the patient, due to feelings of stress and persecution. These feelings can be linked to a number of symptoms of schizophrenia but in particular hallucinations and paranoia.

An early study into the connection between high expressed emotion and relapse in patients with schizophrenia was conducted by Brown et al. (1972). They studied 101 patients who had previously been admitted to a hospital with symptoms of schizophrenia and had since been returned to the family home. They used interviews with family members to establish the level of expressed emotion in the family and categorised 45 as high EE and 56 as low EE. They found that of the 35 who had suffered a relapse, 29 were living in an environment with a high level of EE. This suggests that a high level of expressed emotion is an important factor in a patient's relapse into schizophrenia.

Question time

What do these theories tell us about the cause of schizophrenia?

What other factors are likely to be involved? Do biological explanations provide a better or worse explanation?

Cognitive explanations for schizophrenia

Cognition means thinking and knowing and, as such, is focused on how we use thoughts to come to understand the world both inside and outside our minds. We use mental processes to come to this understanding and, as has been seen in the study of the psychopathology of depression, faulty thought processing can cause significant problems in our perception of the world around us. Thought processes can be regarded as maladaptive when they fail to help us adjust appropriately to the environment or situation in which we find ourselves.

Beck and Rector (2005) identify a number of factors that contribute to maladaptive thought processes, including neurological impairment, aversive life events and stress reactions. These factors combine to create cognitive biases in the individual and are responsible for both the positive and negative symptoms of schizophrenia.

Positive symptoms are related to a range of biases but one of these is inadequate cognitive processing such as jumping to conclusions. This can help to explain both delusions and hallucinations, as the individual comes to the conclusion that other people are persecuting them or that the voices in their head belong to someone else.

Negative symptoms may be regarded as a form of defence against the negative belief system that they are experiencing, e.g. if I'm going to fail then it's better not to try. The negative symptoms could also be a form of defence against the positive symptoms that they are experiencing, because withdrawal and disengagement may help to protect them from the fears that arise from the experience of delusions and hallucinations.

Dysfunctional thought processes can alter our perception and lead to problems in the extent to which we feel in control of our behaviour. Frith (1979) suggested that these dysfunctional thought processes are caused by a failure of cognitive inhibition in which stimuli that normally occur below the level of consciousness and are filtered out are breaking through, resulting in the person being exposed to a mass of irrelevant information. As a consequence of this, there are difficulties in processing and interpreting all of the information. This inability can relate to a range of schizophrenic symptoms. For example, hallucinations might result from the perception of sounds that normally wouldn't reach the conscious level; and delusions might result from an attempt to explain and interpret the source of the irrelevant information that has broken through into consciousness. Faulty interpretations of this sort can lead to problems in recognising what is coming from the person themselves and what is coming from elsewhere, so the person might come to regard their own thoughts as coming from elsewhere alongside the mass of other sounds that are breaking through into consciousness.

In later years, Frith and Done (1988) modified this explanation as the idea of a defective filter wasn't being supported by experimental evidence. They introduced an explanation that focused on defects in the interpretation of output, rather than input. Rather than trying to explain auditory hallucinations as misinterpretations of stimuli coming from elsewhere, they suggested that they were caused by misinterpretations of stimuli coming from the person, e.g. talking to yourself. According to this view, the problem is caused by a breakdown in the internal monitoring system that would normally monitor thoughts and actions (metacognition) and tell a person not only when they are about to occur but also the source of those thoughts and actions. This breakdown causes thoughts and actions to be seen as 'alien' and therefore not under the individual's control, which can then be applied to auditory hallucinations and delusions of control.

Further problems with cognitive processes relate to understanding the intentions of other people and comes from the area of social cognition. There appear to be problems in the theory of mind of individuals with schizophrenia, which is the ability to correctly interpret other people's thoughts or, if you prefer, to read the minds of other people is impaired. This inability can lead someone to incorrectly predict the behaviour of others and to regard them as dangerous, creating obvious links with paranoia.

Question time

What do these theories tell us about the causes of schizophrenia?
Do they explain all of the symptoms of schizophrenia?
Is there anything missing from these explanations?

Mini plenary

Connect the list of terms below with the appropriate definition by drawing a line from the correct term to the correct definition:

Term	Definition
Double bind	A failure of cognitive inhibition in which irrelevant stimuli break through, causing confusion.
Cognitive biases	Parental interactions are contradictory in that they are giving their children mixed messages, leaving the young person confused about how to react.
Expressed emotion	Criticism and hostility directed towards the patient by family members, combined with emotional over-involvement in the life of the patient.
Dysfunctional thought processes	Inadequate cognitive processing and a negative belief system.

AO2 (Application of knowledge): How does this apply in practice?

Interleave me now

Holism, reductionism and explanations for mental disorders

Any attempt to explain a disorder or illness can be analysed in terms of whether it provides an overly simple or indeed overly complex explanation. If it provides an overly simple explanation, it could be accused of not taking other influential factors into account. If it provides an overly complex explanation however, it could be accused of not being useful as it is difficult to apply to specific circumstances. Some explanations for mental disorders could be regarded as reductionist, for example those that rely purely on biological factors as the cause of the disorder (e.g. biological explanations for OCD). Others might be regarded as holist (e.g. humanist explanations for depression).

Holism and reductionism in relation to family dysfunction explanations

At first sight, an explanation that purely focuses on the family as a source of the problems experienced by those with schizophrenia could be seen as reductionist as it only focuses on that one factor and fails to take into account the range of other possible factors that could bring on the disorder. However, the family dysfunction explanations provided above are not being put forward as a cause as such, but more as a risk factor and if we regard the many other factors that have been put forward as explanations in the same way, i.e. as just more risk factors, then the argument could be seen as much more holist than any other. In fact, with this in mind, the reductionist explanations could be those that attempt to explain schizophrenia solely in terms of single factors, e.g. genetics.

One theory that has sometimes been mistakenly put forward as reductionist was that of R.D. Laing (1965) who has been accused in the past of blaming parents for causing the symptoms of schizophrenia in their children. However, this accusation doesn't take into account that Laing was actually arguing that schizophrenia wasn't a real illness and therefore didn't need treatment. He suggested that what the medical profession regards as a mental illness was nothing more than behaviour developed in response to certain forms of treatment within the family. Therefore it could be seen as an argument against the reductionism of the psychiatric profession's attempts to explain schizophrenia as a biological phenomenon that should only be treated using biological methods, such as drugs.

Think!

Is it holist or reductionist to explain the symptoms of schizophrenia in the way that Laing did?

What are the implications for treatment, if we accept Laing's view?

Interleave me now

Cognition and memory

One of the areas of psychology that is explained by the cognitive approach is how we use mental processes to retain information about events that have happened in the past. In other words, our memory. One of the important features in the study of memory is the notion of schemas, which are mental representations of all of the knowledge we have about a certain topic or situation. They are formed from our experiences and provide us with information to help us recognise things we have come into contact with in the past as well as things we may come into contact with in the future. We can compare new experiences against these schemas in order to work out how we should respond and are therefore extremely important in our day-to-day understanding of the world around us.

Memory, schemas and schizophrenia

According to Hemsley (1993), schizophrenia arises when there is an impairment in the normal process of making sense of current input, using our understanding of past regularities (schemas) in behaviour and situations. If we are unable to make sense of current sensory input using schemas, then we may try to make sense of it in some other way. If we are trying to understand all new inputs without the influence of past experiences, then we may have problems inferring the cause of behaviour based purely on this single occurrence.

Imagine going through life without the knowledge that you have built up through the various experiences you have had, like a small child or an alien from another planet! Sensory experiences will all be novel, and you will need to come to a decision about what it is and what is causing it to happen quickly, and without the use of previous knowledge. Think of how a small child might interpret auditory stimuli they have never heard before in a particular context, such as a creaking floorboard, as strange and possibly coming from an unusual source, like a ghost or a monster. The impaired schizophrenic mind can come to interpret stimuli as coming from an unusual source, and this can lead to strange attributions that make no sense to someone familiar with the context.

This shows how important schemas and the context in which stimuli occur are for a rational understanding of what is happening in the world around us and within our own minds. Without these past regularities, our perception can become irregular and disordered, leading to the perception of hallucinations and delusions.

Think!

How do you use memory schemas in your everyday life?

How important are they in your understanding of current events?

How does this relate to schizophrenia?

Mini plenary

Elaine has been diagnosed with schizophrenia after a number of incidents in which she stopped traffic on a road near her house because voices in her head told her that the cars were trying to cause her harm by polluting the area in which she lived.

How would a cognitive psychologist explain Elaine's behaviour?

AO3 (Analysis and evaluation of knowledge): How useful are these explanations?

Why is there a problem with causation in psychological explanations?

The problem of causation is one that continually rears its head in explanations for schizophrenia, as was shown in Chapter 3 when looking at biological explanations. Although it is a problem to establish the direction of cause in biological explanations, it is just as difficult in psychological explanations.

Family dysfunction has been identified as a possible risk factor in schizophrenia and also as a possible source of relapse. It could be that being in a home with overly involved family members may cause those with schizophrenia to relapse, but it could equally be the case that the difficulties of having someone in the home who may still be displaying the symptoms of schizophrenia might cause family members to be heavily involved and to become protective, thus making it difficult to establish which was the cause and which the effect. It would be extremely unethical to create situations in which someone were exposed to the kind of double bind behaviour outlined above just to see if they developed schizophrenic symptoms, consequently we are reliant on showing that the type of behaviour identified is prevalent in the families of people with schizophrenia but this still doesn't tell us whether this was the cause or effect of schizophrenia.

However, in the case of cognitive explanations, it is possible to conduct experiments to compare the thought processes of non-schizophrenics with those of schizophrenics to attempt to provide experimental evidence to show cause and effect. Waters et al. (2010) conducted a meta-analysis of such experiments covering a 30-year period and found significant evidence that self-recognition deficits were so common in schizophrenics as compared to non-schizophrenics that it was almost possible to establish a causal relationship. However, the thinking patterns that are being displayed may just as easily be the result of having schizophrenia as be the cause and so, in spite of this evidence, it is extremely difficult to be able to accurately identify which came first.

> **Think!**
>
> Do you think that the kind of experimental evidence referred to above shows the cause of schizophrenia?

Is there a connection between cognitive dysfunction and neurological problems?

The argument that cognitive explanations don't identify the origin of the problem and as such are incomplete is one that has been put forward regularly in response to the kinds of dysfunctional thought processes outlined above. However, this ignores the large body of research that has been able to establish a link between cognitive dysfunction and neurological problems in those with schizophrenia.

Frith et al. (2000), reported studies, e.g. Spence et al. (1997), that had shown connections between abnormal activity in sections of the brain such as the superior parietal cortex and the kind of cognitive deficits identified by himself and others. These connections have been further supported by studies that have attempted to show neural correlates with self-monitoring and self-reflection from which various areas of the brain have been identified as possible sources of these cognitive dysfunctions.

Advances in cognitive neuroscience have meant that it is very difficult to continue to argue that cognitive psychologists don't account for the origin of the dysfunctions identified, as many of them are now working within this field and are clearly looking to the connection between the brain and such cognitive problems.

However, it has not been easy to identify a brain abnormality that has been consistently correlated with these dysfunctions, nor has it been easy to identify an area of the brain that can be consistently correlated with schizophrenia in general. This was noted by Frith (1992) in his book *Cognitive Neuropsychology of Schizophrenia*, in which he notes that he has 'known neuropathologists to remark facetiously that it is easy to recognise the brains from schizophrenic patients because they are the ones which look normal'.

This suggests that the criticism of cognitive psychology as being unable to identify the origin of the problem is still justified in spite of many efforts to do so.

What is the influence of neurodevelopmental factors in schizophrenia?

Attempts to identify family dysfunction and cognitive impairments as the causes of schizophrenia have both encountered significant problems and have thus fallen short of a complete explanation. Even the attempt to combine cognitive and neurological evidence has continued to prove problematic. Consequently, it may be necessary to consider an interaction of environmental and genetic factors to provide a fuller explanation.

In research supported by the Medical Research Council (MRC), Owen et al. (2011), have suggested that one of the difficulties that has arisen in trying to identify specific brain abnormalities or specific cognitive impairments is that the characteristic symptoms of schizophrenia actually result from a syndrome that is more generally related to neurodevelopmental disorders such as autism, attention deficit hyperactivity disorder (ADHD) and intellectual disability. They argue that these syndromes should all be seen as resulting, at least in part, from a combination of genetic and environmental effects on brain development that are associated with specific and general impairments of cognitive function.

It is their argument that just as the overlap between schizophrenia and bipolar disorder has been established, we should now be looking at the overlapping symptoms of the neurodevelopmental syndromes mentioned above to see the level of comorbidity involved. They further argue that there are other connections that should be made, e.g. they are all more common in males, they are all associated with developmental delay and motor abnormalities, and they all involve some form of cognitive impairment. They argue that such disorders need to be seen as part of a continuum with varying degrees of brain abnormalities and varying severity of environmental effects influencing where an individual might fall on the continuum.

The implications of this argument are to suggest that there should be stronger connections between the different organisations looking to treat these disorders and consequently for a change in the approach to treatment.

> **Think!**
>
> How would this explanation affect how we think about schizophrenia? What might it change?

What are the ethical implications of identifying family dysfunction as the cause of schizophrenia?

There are many forms of research that have come to be regarded as socially sensitive in the area of abnormal development because of the effect that they have had on the individuals who are suffering with the disorders. However, family dysfunction explanations can also have ethical implications for the families of those suffering as they have the potential to shift the blame for the cause of the disorder on to the families themselves.

This 'blame the parents' approach can be a major problem for the families of individuals with schizophrenia and only serves to add to the pressure felt by such families. This may in turn cause the families to feel the need to 'do something' about their son's/daughter's disorder and behave in ways that might be regarded as unhelpful or even dysfunctional.

Therefore, the ethical implications may lead on to practical implications, prolong the course of the disorder, and even lead to relapse. This suggests that expressed emotion may well be a factor in the relapse of individuals with schizophrenia but the reason for the expressed emotion may actually come from the pressure that comes from the stigma of blame rather than from the pressure of having someone with schizophrenia in the family.

Question time

What are the alternatives to the psychological explanations outlined in this chapter?

Are these alternatives likely to be enough on their own to explain schizophrenia?

Are these alternatives better or worse than psychological explanations? Can they be seen as complementary?

Mini plenary

Using the evaluation points above, try to evaluate the following statement:

Psychological factors alone are sufficient to explain the development of schizophrenia.

Arguments for	Arguments against

A modern issue: can we use virtual reality to recreate the experience of schizophrenia?

One of the problems faced by those trying to explain and treat schizophrenia is that it may not be practical or ethical to recreate the experience of schizophrenia in real settings. However, it may be that advances in technology such as the use of virtual reality may now make this a possibility and open up the chance to see the world from the point of view of the person with schizophrenia.

New research

MED-TECH INNOVATION NEWS

Five ways virtual reality is transforming mental health

13 May 2019

The article looks at how the development of virtual reality has enabled those providing psychotherapy a new tool to improve the experience of therapy, particularly for those with schizophrenia. VR-enabled therapy is able to provide a digitally created environment with tasks for the patients to complete that are personally designed for them. In the article, it is argued that there are five key benefits to the new approach.

1. The therapy is providing better outcomes than face-to-face sessions as it is able to help patients with the fears and inhibitions they may experience when dealing with someone face-to-face.
2. It creates the possibility of treating a larger number of patients due to the fact that the therapist is embedded in the system as an avatar and so can treat many patients at one time.
3. The technology can provide a better experience for patients as it is so powerful and realistic that it becomes fun as well as effective and patients find it easier to engage with.

4. There is a great possibility for cutting costs as the technology can be used again and again, even though there are some upfront costs, the fact that it takes the place of many individuals means that it saves money in the long term.
5. In the modern world, patients expect more advanced forms of treatment and this can be used effectively with younger patients too. On the whole, the experience is generally regarded as pleasant and positive.

Question time

What does this article tell us about the treatment of schizophrenia?

How do you think it could be used to recreate psychological factors like family dysfunction and dysfunctional thought processes?

Are there any problems with the use of virtual reality for the treatment of schizophrenia?

Chapter plenary

1. How do psychological factors influence mental health?
2. What are the two types of psychological explanations for schizophrenia?
3. What is meant by family dysfunction?
4. What is the double bind theory of schizophrenia?
5. What is the expressed emotion theory of schizophrenia?
6. What is meant by cognitive explanations in relation to schizophrenia?
7. What is meant by cognitive biases in relation to schizophrenia?
8. What is meant by dysfunctional thought processing in relation to schizophrenia?
9. How does the holism and reductionism debate apply to schizophrenia?
10. How do memory and schemas apply to schizophrenia?
11. Why is there a problem with causation in psychological explanations?
12. Is there a connection between cognitive dysfunction and neurological problems in the development of schizophrenia?
13. What is the influence of neurodevelopmental factors in schizophrenia?
14. What are the ethical implications of identifying family dysfunction as the cause of schizophrenia?
15. How can the use of virtual reality help in the treatment of schizophrenia?

Glossary

Key word	Definition
Adaptive	Something that aids normal functioning.
Cognitive biases	An error in thinking that affects the decisions that people make.
Cognitive inhibition	The mind's ability to tune out irrelevant stimuli.
Double bind theory	Parents sending out contradictory messages that create confusion in a child/family member.
Dysfunctional thought processes	Information processing that is not working properly and producing undesirable consequences.
Expressed emotion	The tendency to make hostile or critical comments to a family member with schizophrenia or to be emotionally over-involved in their life.
Family dysfunction	A family in which conflict is normal.
Flat affect	A lack of emotional response, e.g. expressionless face.
Holist	The most complex explanation that tries to look at the complete picture to explain behaviour and explore all of the factors that might influence it.
Maladaptive	Something that prevents normal functioning.
Meta-analysis	The examination of data taken from a number of sources to attempt to show patterns or trends.
Metacognition	Self-monitoring of thoughts and actions.
Neurodevelopmental disorders	Impairments of the growth and development of the brain.
Problem of causation	The difficulty in knowing whether something is the cause or effect of something else.
Reductionist	The simplest explanation that seeks to find a single cause for behaviour.
Schemas	A mental framework that informs someone of what to expect in certain situations.
Schizophrenogenic mother	A term first used by Fromm-Reichmann in 1948 to describe a mother who would display both rejecting and controlling behaviour towards their child. This became a stereotype for the mother of someone with schizophrenia, but has largely been rejected in recent times.
Self-recognition deficits	A person's inability to recognise something as coming from themselves, e.g. their own thoughts.

Key word	Definition
Superior parietal cortex	A section of the brain that is involved with spatial orientation.
Theory of mind	The ability to understand that other people have their own thoughts and feelings.

Plenary: Exam-style questions and answers with advisory comments

Question 1.

Explain what is meant by dysfunctional thought processing in relation to schizophrenia. [4 marks]

Marks for this question: AO1 = 4

Advice: In a question like this, it's important to make sure you are clearly explaining the link between the dysfunctional thoughts and schizophrenia. This question might be difficult as it is easy to fall into the trap of over-explaining, so you need to make sure your explanation is concise. There is no need to provide any analysis or evaluation as all of the marks are for AO1: Knowledge and understanding.

Possible answer: The cognitive approach to schizophrenia explains the disorder with reference to problems with information processing and one example of that is dysfunctional thought processes. These can occur when there is a failure of cognitive inhibition so that a person finds it difficult to filter out what they need from the mass of information that is coming into their mind. If they have a defective filter, then they may become overloaded and they misinterpret information coming from elsewhere as coming from in their head, leading to the perception of auditory hallucinations. Another issue is that that someone may have a problem with monitoring their own thoughts and actions, leading to a problem with metacognition as they are unable to accurately identify the source of their thoughts and actions. This can lead to both hallucinations and delusions of control as they see their own thoughts and actions as coming from or being controlled by another source.

Question 2.

Describe and evaluate psychological explanations for schizophrenia. [16 marks]

Marks for this question: AO1 = 6 and AO3 = 10

Advice: This question asks for explanations (plural) so must include more than one explanation. Therefore, it is probably best to provide both cognitive and family dysfunction explanations. The question is looking for both skills of knowledge and understanding and analysis and evaluation. As there are 6 marks for AO1 and 10 for AO3, there should be greater emphasis on the evaluation. However, all such extended writing questions are marked holistically and therefore it is important that the knowledge is accurate and detailed and that the evaluation is clear and effective.

Possible answer: Psychological explanations include a variety of influences ranging from specific environmental factors that have an influence on us and alter our behaviour to factors that are directly related to mental processes and affect our understanding of the world around us. All these factors can affect our normal daily lives through their influence on our thoughts and feelings, which may sometimes be *adaptive* but at times can be *maladaptive* too.

One area that can cause a problem is family dysfunction and, in particular, the dysfunctional communication systems that are sometimes used within families. One example of this is the double-bind theory put forward by Bateson et al., which is characterised by contradictory messages being given out by parents, as they sometimes put their children in a no-win situation. Bateson et al. suggest that parents may have feelings of hostility towards their children and so try to make up for this by behaving in a loving way. Unfortunately their hostility will still come out so they may encourage loving behaviour, e.g. 'come here and give me a hug', but then reject the child as their hostility comes to the fore, e.g. 'get off me you soppy fool'. This leaves the child confused and paranoid as they find it hard to trust their parent.

Another example of dysfunctional communication comes when the person with schizophrenia is back in the family home and trying to recover from the disorder. Family members may become emotionally over-involved in the life of the recovering person and try too hard to make sure they are all right by constantly asking them if they're okay or by trying to do things for them. Alternatively, they may become highly critical of the behaviour of the recovering person and show high levels of expressed emotion, leading to conflict and the possibility that the person will relapse into schizophrenia as they begin to feel stressed and persecuted.

Cognitive explanations focus on faulty information processing as the cause of schizophrenia. A person may have a problem with cognitive inhibition caused by a defective filter, which can make them become overloaded with sensory information and find it difficult to interpret what is coming from them and what from elsewhere. This can lead to the perception of auditory hallucinations. Further problems arise as the normal process of metacognition is disrupted and they are unable to accurately monitor their own thoughts and actions. This may lead to confusion about the source of these thoughts and actions and to delusions of control if they believe their actions and thoughts are being controlled by someone/something else.

One problem with family dysfunction explanations is that there is a problem with causation. It isn't easy to establish whether communication problems such as expressed emotion in the family are the cause of the relapse back into schizophrenia or are caused by having a person with schizophrenia in the family. It must be hard for everyone in this situation and it could be that having a family member with schizophrenia makes it difficult to carry on as normal. In spite of a parent's best efforts to care for and look after their child, they are then accused of being emotionally over-involved and the cause of the relapse, which hardly seems fair. The pressure of this blame may actually lead to behaviour that is unhelpful or even dysfunctional, and that could be the cause of the relapse rather than anything else.

Similarly, it could be that faulty information processing could just as easily be the result of having schizophrenia as the cause of the problem. However, Waters et al. conducted a meta-analysis of experiments covering a 30-year period and found significant evidence that self-recognition deficits were so common in schizophrenics as compared to non-schizophrenics that it was almost possible to establish a causal relationship. This suggests that causation may be more easily identified in cognitive explanations than in family dysfunction explanations.

Another area of evaluation that seems to be relevant to family dysfunction is that it could be seen as reductionist, as it seems to purely be blaming the family for the problems faced by the person with schizophrenia. However, it should be noted that this dysfunction is being put forward as a risk factor in the development of schizophrenia, rather than a cause and as such can be seen as one risk factor among many and therefore not reductionist, unlike the biological explanations, which focus purely on single factors like genes as the cause of schizophrenia.

Cognitive explanations are also difficult to accuse of reductionism as they incorporate both mental processes and neurological evidence. Spence et al. showed connections between abnormal activity in sections of the brain such as the superior parietal cortex and the kinds of cognitive deficits identified above. These connections have been further supported by studies that have attempted to show neural correlates with self-monitoring and self-reflection from which various areas of the brain have been identified as possible sources of these cognitive dysfunctions. However, Frith notes that he has known neuropathologists to remark that it is easy to recognise the brains from schizophrenic patients because they are the ones that look normal, suggesting that it isn't always so easy to identify these neurological issues and possibly the question of where cognitive dysfunctions come from requires an even more holistic approach.

Further problems in trying to identify the source of cognitive deficits in schizophrenia have come from research supported by the Medical Research Council, which suggests that one of the difficulties that has arisen in trying to identify specific brain abnormalities or specific cognitive impairments is that the characteristic symptoms of schizophrenia actually result from a syndrome that is more generally related to *neurodevelopmental disorders* such as autism, ADHD and intellectual disability. They argue that these syndromes should all be seen as resulting, at least in part, from a combination of genetic and environmental effects on brain development that are associated with specific and general impairments of cognitive function. This creates the problem of comorbidity and symptom overlap, which means that it is virtually impossible to separate one disorder from another and has important implications for how we treat schizophrenia.

References

Bateson, G., Jackson, D.D., Haley, J. and Weakland, J. (1956). The double bind. *Behavioral Science*, 1 (4): 251–254.

Beck, A.T. and Rector, N.A. (2005) Cognitive approaches to schizophrenia: Theory and therapy. *Annual Review of Clinical Psychology*, 1: 577–606.

Bolland, I. (2019) Five ways technology is transforming mental health. *Med-Tech Innovation News*, 13 May 2019.

Brown, G.W., Birley, J.L. and Wing, J.K. (1972) Influence of family life on the course of schizophrenic disorders: A replication. *The British Journal of Psychiatry*, 121 (562): 241–258.

Frith, C.D. (1979) Consciousness, information processing and schizophrenia. *The British Journal of Psychiatry*, 134 (3): 225–235.

Frith, C.D. (1992) *The Cognitive Neuropsychology of Schizophrenia*. Hove, UK: Psychology Press.

Frith, C.D. and Done, D.J. (1988) Towards a neuropsychology of schizophrenia. *The British Journal of Psychiatry*, 153 (4): 437–443.

Frith, C.D., Blakemore, S.J. and Wolpert, D.M. (2000) Explaining the symptoms of schizophrenia: Abnormalities in the awareness of action. *Brain Research Reviews*, 31 (2–3): 357–363.

Hemsley, D.R. (1993) A simple (or simplistic?) cognitive model for schizophrenia. *Behaviour Research and Therapy*, 31 (7): 633–645.

Laing, R.D. (1965) The divided self: An existential study in sanity and madness. Harmondsworth, UK: Penguin Books.

Owen, M.J., O'Donovan, M.C., Thapar, A. and Craddock, N. (2011) Neurodevelopmental hypothesis of schizophrenia. *The British Journal of Psychiatry*, 198 (3): 173–175.

Spence, S.A., Brooks, D.J., Hirsch, S.R., Liddle, P.F., Meehan, J. and Grasby, P.M. (1997) A PET study of voluntary movement in schizophrenic patients experiencing passivity phenomena (delusions of alien control). *Brain: A Journal of Neurology*, 120 (11): 1997–2011.

Waters, F., Woodward, T., Allen, P., Aleman, A. and Sommer, I. (2010). Self-recognition deficits in schizophrenia patients with auditory hallucinations: A meta-analysis of the literature. *Schizophrenia Bulletin*, 38 (4): 741–750.

Chapter 5
Biological treatments for schizophrenia

Spec check

Drug therapy: typical and atypical antipsychotics.

AO1 (Knowledge and understanding): What are the biological treatments for schizophrenia?

Why use drugs to treat schizophrenia?

The biological explanations for schizophrenia discussed in Chapter 3 suggested that schizophrenia was associated with factors that affected the balance of a person's biological make-up. The genetic explanation suggested that there may be a gene or, more likely, a combination of genes that affect a person's mental state and that at least some (if not all) of these genes are related to the balance of neurotransmitters in a person's body. The neural correlates explanation suggested that the brain and nervous system are affected in a way that forms of activity in the brain cause the person to show the symptoms of schizophrenia. The dopamine hypothesis is very clearly linked to the balance of neurotransmitters as it suggests that levels of the neurotransmitter dopamine are responsible for the symptoms of schizophrenia.

The evidence seems to suggest that schizophrenia is at least associated with (if not caused by) biological processes that are linked to the chemical balance in the body and, as such, it would seem logical to suggest that a way to deal with these might be to change the chemical balance. The introduction of drugs that will help to change that chemical balance would therefore seem to be a way forward in the treatment of those with schizophrenia. Such drugs are called psychotropic drugs and they work by changing or balancing the quantity of neurotransmitters in the brain. The main chemical that has been associated with schizophrenia is dopamine, which is the neurotransmitter usually targeted by these drugs.

Think!

If you had found that there was an association between dopamine levels and schizophrenia and you had a drug that could alter those dopamine levels, what would you do?

Would you give someone the drug, even if you weren't sure it was the actual cause of the problem?

Typical antipsychotics

These drugs, also referred to as conventional or first-generation antipsychotics, have been around since the 1950s and have a long history not just for treating psychosis but also as a sedative, as they have sometimes been used to treat acute cases of nervousness before surgical operations, and even to treat prolonged and excessive cases of hiccups. This neuroleptic effect was the first aspect of the use of these drugs to be discovered and, according to Ramachandraiah et al. (2009), was discovered by a French army surgeon called Laborit in 1949, when being used as a sedative to treat surgical shock. He then campaigned for their use as a psychiatric therapy throughout the early 1950s. However, this effect was later regarded as secondary to the effect on dopaminergic transmission, which was believed to be more of an issue in the therapeutic use of the drugs.

An example of a typical antipsychotic is the drug chlorpromazine, which can be taken as a tablet, syrup or injection depending on the severity and speed of action required. Most patients will be prescribed the tablet form in small doses of 50–75 mg per day initially, working up to around 400 mg per day in the long term. The drug is particularly noted for its effectiveness in the treatment of mania symptoms that are associated with schizophrenia, particularly hallucinations.

Chlorpromazine is one of a class of drugs called phenothiazines, which work as antagonists for a number of neurotransmitter receptors, including dopamine, and leads to the reduction of the action of dopamine by blocking its receptors at the synapse. The effect of this reduction is to balance out levels of dopamine in the important areas of the brain identified by the dopamine hypothesis in Chapter 3. Unfortunately, these typical antipsychotics were found to have extrapyramidal side effects, such as tardive dyskinesia and, even worse, neuroleptic malignant syndrome (NMS), consequently the need for a drug with less serious side effects was identified.

Atypical antipsychotics

The search for a drug with less severe side effects as well as for a drug to treat those who seemed to be resistant to typical antipsychotics led to the use of a class of drugs referred to as atypical/unconventional or sometimes second-generation antipsychotics. The notion of atypical comes from the idea that they are not typical because they don't have the same extrapyramidal side effects as the typical antipsychotics. These drugs were developed as part of a process of working with tricyclic compounds that had been used in the treatment of depression to introduce drugs that worked on both the positive and negative symptoms of schizophrenia.

Clozapine is an atypical antipsychotic that was developed in the 1960s as part of the process outlined above and was found to have effective neuroleptic properties without the side effects associated with chlorpromazine. Clozapine works in a similar way to chlorpromazine by blocking dopamine receptors but does this more weakly than chlorpromazine by only temporarily blocking these receptors (Kapur and Remington, 2001), which may help to explain the lack of extrapyramidal side effects. However, clozapine has also been found to have an effect on negative symptoms of schizophrenia such as avolition and apathy, as well as having an effect on mood and cognition, therefore, it seems to have an effect on other neurotransmitters, e.g. serotonin and glutamate.

Clozapine has not been without its own problems and, due to the discovery in the 1970s that one of the side effects of the drug is agranulocytosis, which had led to a number of deaths of those using it, the use of the drug was withdrawn. However, due to the demands of psychiatrists for its return and later discoveries that if the use of the drug was monitored in the early stages, these problems could be avoided, the drug was reintroduced in the 1980s alongside regular blood tests being taken when the drug is being used. Furthermore, the drug can be given in lower doses than chlorpromazine, typically starting at 25–50 mg per day, up to around 300 mg per day but it is still found to be more effective.

Another atypical antipsychotic that has been developed, partially due to the need to avoid the serious side effects of clozapine, is risperidone, which affects both dopamine and serotonin receptors and reduces the activity of both. Risperidone was developed in the 1990s and has a stronger action than clozapine for dopamine and serotonin receptors meaning that the drug can be used in lower doses than clozapine, typically starting with 4–8 mg per day, up to around 12 mg per day. Like clozapine, risperidone only binds to dopamine receptors temporarily, so that the risk of extrapyramidal side effects is still low, but it has also been found that there is a significant risk of side effects if the dose goes over 16 mg per day (Marder and Meibach, 1994). Although atypical antipsychotics have been associated with metabolism problems and weight gain, risperidone is thought to be the safest atypical antipsychotic drug, particularly in relation to metabolic syndrome (Guatam and Meena, 2011).

Question time

Why use drugs to treat schizophrenia?

What does drug treatment suggest about the causes of schizophrenia?

Are there any problems with using drugs to treat schizophrenia?

Identify the similarities and differences between the typical and atypical antipsychotics.

	Similarities	Differences
Typical and atypical antipsychotic drugs		

AO2 (Application of knowledge): How does this apply in practice?

Interleave me now

Ethical issues

Treating schizophrenia has always been a controversial issue as it is a mental disorder that isn't always reliably diagnosed (see Chapter 2), isn't easily explained (see Chapters 3 and 4) and isn't always recognised as something that needs treatment by those that have it. This leads to the question of whether we have the right to force people to undergo treatment, particularly when that treatment is one that will involve strong psychotropic drugs being introduced into their system. Further issues arise when we consider that the use of such drugs may be more for the benefit of others than for the person suffering, as the drugs can make them easier for us to cope with and less likely to cause difficulties. This is why some have referred to antipsychotic drugs as nothing more than chemical straitjackets.

The question of consent

Although you may have studied consent, you will probably have only looked at it in relation to the use of human participants in research, but now we are looking at consent as an issue in medical treatment. While the issue of informed consent does apply to medical practice, the General Medical Council (GMC) has guidelines that explain that in order for consent to be valid, the medical staff must provide information that is full and honest (GMC, 1998). This is also true in cases of mental illness, unless it has been decided that the patient is a danger to themselves and others and possibly has been detained under section 3 of the Mental Health Act (1983), in which case it isn't necessary to have consent from the patient, although it is always preferable to try to obtain it. This has been added to by the Mental Health Act (2007) and Community Treatment Orders have been introduced, which allow for patients to be treated without consent in the community or in hospital.

The use of antipsychotics has become even more of an issue in recent years as the use of them has grown in the UK and the USA. According to Moncrieff (2013) antipsychotics 'have become the most costly class of drug treatment used for mental health problems in England', which gives an indication of how prevalent is their use. The National Institute for Clinical Excellence (NICE) allows for their short-term use with any agitated patients, and this includes patients with dementia, for whom the drugs were never intended but with whom the use is now widespread. This is regarded by many as an abuse of human rights, although decisions in court have gone against this and decided that as long as the responsible medical officer has decided that the treatment is necessary and that the side effects are not too severe then the patient can be given the medication without consent (PS, R, 2003).

Think!

Do you think that patients should be given drugs without their consent? If so, in what circumstances should it be done?

Does this go against their human rights? Should human rights considerations come before medical considerations?

Interleave me now

Biopsychology and neurotransmitters

In the study of biopsychology, we are considering how the central nervous system (CNS, the brain and spinal cord) influences behaviour and the importance of communication within the CNS for our normal functioning. You will have seen how the process of communication is both an electrical and chemical one, that neurotransmitters are involved in this process and that neurons contain receptors that are specialised for particular neurotransmitters such as dopamine.

Neurotransmitters and antipsychotic drugs

In the normal process of synaptic transmission, neurons transmit signals electrically along their axons and the synapses (junctions between neurons) transmit the signals chemically to the next neuron. Normally when an action potential reaches the axon terminal, vesicles release neurotransmitters into the synaptic cleft, the neurotransmitters bind to receptors on the post-synaptic neuron and activate them, enzymes are released to break down the neurotransmitter and any neurotransmitter that is not received by the post-synaptic neuron is taken back up by the pre-synaptic neuron (re-uptake).

However, when antipsychotic drugs such as chlorpromazine are taken, the process is prevented by the psychoactive ingredients in these drugs binding to the dopamine receptors without activating them and thereby blocking the activity of dopamine.

This blockade of dopamine receptors is likely to be compensated for by the brain increasing the number or density of dopamine receptors and possibly creating supersensitivity to dopamine in the person receiving the antipsychotics, which can then lead to more serious side effects.

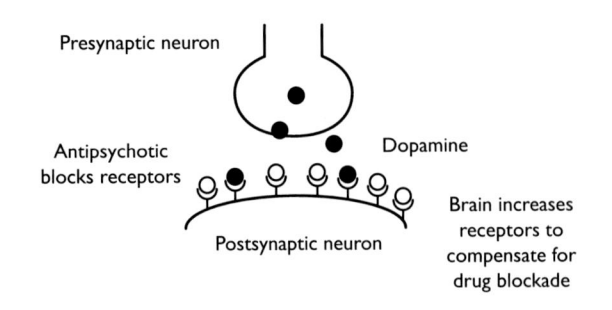

Dopamine function after exposure to antipsychotics

Figure 5.1 The effect of antipsychotics on dopamine function

Question time

What does this tell us about how antipsychotics work?

Does this model suggest that antipsychotics are likely to be effective?

Why might they not be effective?

Mini plenary

A friend of yours has been diagnosed with schizophrenia and his family have asked you if you know anything about the treatment he might receive.

Explain the use of antipsychotics in a way that your friend's family can understand. Try to make it understandable by people who aren't doctors or scientists.

AO3 (Analysis and evaluation of knowledge): How useful are these treatments?

What problems are caused by the side effects of antipsychotics?

The side effects of antipsychotic medication are well documented and numerous, with problems related to stiffness, restlessness, sexual problems and weight gain being among the effects most associated with the drugs.

Typical antipsychotics such as chlorpromazine have been particularly associated with tardive dyskinesia, which involves the patient displaying involuntary movements of the mouth, lips and jaw and, even more seriously, neuroleptic malignant syndrome, which involves a very high fever, accelerated heart rate, autonomic nervous system dysfunction and even death. It seems as though typical antipsychotics block dopamine activity in the hypothalamus, which affects autonomic function and leads to problems in a number of areas of normal functioning.

Although atypical antipsychotics were introduced as a way of lessening these effects, they are still associated with significant side effects, in particular agranulocytosis, which is a reduction in the white blood cells that are needed by the body to fight off infections, and which has been particularly associated with clozapine.

The problems caused by these side effects, apart from the obvious dangers to a person's normal health, are that patients may feel as though they are better off with the symptoms of schizophrenia, rather than having to endure the many effects outlined above. Even those that might seem relatively minor, such as weight gain, may be just the sort of thing that will make patients want to avoid taking these drugs – and go to extreme lengths to avoid doing so. One of the risks related to this situation is the potential for patients to consider suicide as they face a future with the choice between the symptoms of schizophrenia or the effects of antipsychotic drugs.

However, it has also been noted that, while schizophrenia is associated with a greater risk of suicide, Pompili et al. (2016) have shown that antipsychotics, and clozapine in particular, have significant anti-suicidal properties.

> **Think!**
>
> Some of the side effects of antipsychotics aren't particularly dangerous. Does this mean they aren't really a problem?

Are antipsychotics an effective treatment?

Many studies have been conducted into the effectiveness of both typical and atypical antipsychotic medication and most of them have indicated that it is effective for a large number of those with schizophrenia and, therefore, this should provide justification for its use.

In a review of over 1,100 records looking into the effectiveness of chlorpromazine, Adams et al. (2014) found that compared to a placebo control group, the drug significantly both reduced relapse rates and improved their symptoms and general functioning, although they also found important side effects, including considerable weight gain.

In a systematic review of atypical drugs in schizophrenia, Bagnall et al. (2003) looked at over 200 studies into the effectiveness of atypical antipsychotics and found that both clozapine and risperidone were more effective than typical antipsychotics in relieving the overall symptoms of schizophrenia and that both had fewer side effects.

A meta-analysis by Leucht et al. (2018) involving over 28,000 patients, mostly with chronic versions of schizophrenia, was able to show that, compared to

30 per cent of the placebo control group, 51 per cent of the antipsychotic medicated group had at least a minimal response and 23 per cent had a good response, compared with 14 per cent in the control group. Other research by Leucht et al. (2012) showed that relapse rates were significantly improved in those taking antipsychotic medication compared to a placebo control group, with 27 per cent of the medicated group suffering a relapse compared to 64 per cent of the placebo group.

However, in a longitudinal study looking into the use of antipsychotic medication over 20 years, Harrow et al. (2014), found that while the drugs were effective in the short term, in the long term the drugs actually led to the prolonging of psychotic symptoms, compared to a control group who did not use the drugs in the long term. This suggests that antipsychotic medication may actually be detrimental with prolonged use and that patients with schizophrenia would be better off not taking it.

The overall pattern shown in these studies is that there are clear benefits for patients in using both typical and atypical antipsychotics but there is also room for caution in the likelihood of side effects and the potential for detrimental effects in the long term.

Is the use of antipsychotics justified by the evidence from the biological explanations?

Biological explanations and, in particular, the dopamine hypothesis have suggested that administering drugs that influence the levels of dopamine in the brain is the way forward in the treatment of schizophrenia. The logic is that if we can see differences in the dopamine pathways of those with schizophrenia then attempting to change this is the best way forward to prevent the suffering that goes with it. However, the logic of this argument is brought into question by the fact that antipsychotics work by blocking dopamine receptors and therefore reducing the levels of dopamine in the brain, which is fine if we accept the original version of the hypothesis (high levels of dopamine are associated with schizophrenia) but not so fine if we accept the second version, which indicated that it can also be associated with low levels of dopamine in other areas of the brain.

Kesby et al. (2018) have suggested that recent research into the connection between dopamine and schizophrenia causes massive problems for the logic of treating patients with drugs that block dopamine. They argue that there is a need to reconsider this treatment in the light of this research. First, they argue that the positive, negative and cognitive symptoms of schizophrenia have been associated with abnormalities in virtually every neurotransmitter system, so the idea of purely responding by reducing dopamine is hardly likely to be effective. Second, they have suggested that the evidence from brain scanning indicates that the symptoms of schizophrenia are linked to abnormalities in different sections of the brain, which also suggests that a simplistic response isn't useful. Finally, they argue that the studies into the effectiveness of antipsychotics referred to above only serves to demonstrate that there are many patients who do not respond well to dopamine-blocking medication and therefore the studies themselves point to the need for a new approach to the treatment of schizophrenia, which could help all of those who are not improved by current antipsychotic medication and who appear to be resistant to its effects.

The conclusion of this is the need to continually reformulate the approach to schizophrenia as our understanding of the disorder evolves and not to rely on outdated treatments that don't fit the findings of modern research nor the needs of patients.

> **Think!**
>
> What would modern research and the needs of patients suggest about new treatments for schizophrenia?

Are antipsychotics making the brain better or worse?

As suggested above, the rationale for using antipsychotics is that the dopamine pathways in the brain aren't working properly so the aim is to make the brain work better by altering the dopamine levels. However, some have argued that, far from making the brain better, antipsychotics are actually damaging the brain. According to Lawrie (2018), it has become clear over the last 20 years that schizophrenia is associated with a significant reduction in brain volume for both grey and white matter. Lawrie provides a review of a number of studies that have looked into this effect and considers whether it is the disorder that is causing this or the use of antipsychotics.

There is a range of anecdotal and experimental evidence pointing to the fact that those being treated for schizophrenia have suffered this loss of volume. Human studies have found reductions in brain volume in patients using antipsychotics over a significant period of time; and animal studies involving both monkeys and rats have found similar effects in those administered antipsychotics when compared with control groups who were not. Unfortunately, the human studies suffered from the effects of attrition and comparisons with animals were unable to rule out the effect of species differences on the results.

Lawrie also quotes research conducted by himself, which has shown that damage to the brain in patients with schizophrenia occurs even without the use of antipsychotics, and that there are a number of other factors related to the reduction in brain volume in people with schizophrenia that have nothing to do with the use of antipsychotics, including the use of cannabis and alcohol. It seems as though the use of these drugs combined with the effects of schizophrenia put patients at increased risk of brain damage. It has also been noted both that those with schizophrenia are significantly more likely to abuse these substances and that schizophrenia seems to create a predisposition to substance abuse (Green and Brown, 2006).

Lawrie concludes by suggesting that the evidence for the brain damaging effects of antipsychotics has not been proved and it is likely that the other factors, in particular, alcohol and cannabis are responsible for the damaging effects seen in those with schizophrenia. Although it is hard to see how this affected the rats and monkeys who probably didn't have the opportunity to partake in such substances in their spare time!

Question time

What do these points suggest about the use of antipsychotics to treat schizophrenia?

What are the alternatives to the use of antipsychotics?

Are these alternatives better or worse than antipsychotics? Can they be seen as complementary?

Mini plenary

Using the evaluation points above, try to identify arguments for and against the use of antipsychotics to treat schizophrenia.

Arguments for	Arguments against

A modern issue: do antipsychotics create zombies?

The use of antipsychotics in the community has been heralded as a way of taking patients with psychotic disorders such as schizophrenia out of the mental hospital and enable them to live a more normal life in the community. However, whether this is the likely outcome is being questioned by the rise in the use of antipsychotics with the elderly and particularly those with dementia.

New research

THE GUARDIAN

Nursing homes turning residents into 'zombies', Aged Care Royal Commission to hear.

Lisa Martin

15 January 2019

In the article, Martin refers to a Royal Commission being heard in Australia that is looking into the use of antipsychotics in homes for the elderly.

The Commission is being heard due to claims that nursing homes are turning elderly patients into 'zombies' with the regular and prolonged use of antipsychotics.

Ian Yates from the council on the ageing is a major critic of their use. 'A lot of families will complain that their mum or dad, although frail, went into residential care still alert and within a month are like a zombie,' Yates said.

A study of 11,500 nursing home residents by the University of Tasmania found that 60 per cent of them are taking psychotropic medication.

It was also found that many of the residents have been taking the drugs for more than 12 months when they should have only been taking them for a few months.

Most staff believe that the drugs are beneficial in dealing with problem behaviour from the residents and were unaware of the major side effects associated with these drugs, particularly the higher risk of falls and the increased likelihood of strokes.

Question time

What does this article tell us about the use of antipsychotics?

What reasons are given for the increased use of medication?

Does this have any implications for the use of antipsychotics for people with schizophrenia?

What is the alternative to this kind of treatment?

Chapter plenary

1. Why use drugs to treat schizophrenia?
2. What are typical antipsychotics?
3. What are atypical antipsychotics?
4. What are the ethical issues in using drugs to treat schizophrenia?
5. Why is there a question about consent?
6. What is the connection between neurotransmitters and antipsychotic drugs?
7. What problems are caused by the side effects of antipsychotics?
8. Are antipsychotics an effective treatment?
9. Is the use of antipsychotics justified by the evidence from biological explanations?
10. Are antipsychotics making the brain better or worse?
11. Do antipsychotics create zombies?

Glossary

Key word	Definition
Antagonist	An effect of a drug that serves to block the activity of a neurotransmitter rather than activating it.
Attrition	A feature of longitudinal studies that is characterised by participants dropping out over a period of time.
Chemical straitjackets	A term used to compare the use of antipsychotics to the use of a jacket that used to be used as a restraint in mental institutions and had the effect of controlling the patient without having any other benefit.
Chlorpromazine	One of a group of drugs that act on the central nervous system and block dopamine as well as having a sedative effect. It is a typical or conventional antipsychotic.
Clozapine	An atypical antipsychotic that works by temporarily blocking dopamine but also impacts on other neurotransmitters, e.g. serotonin.
Extrapyramidal side effects	Physical symptoms, including tremor, slurred speech and tardive dyskinesia, that are primarily associated with improper dosing of or unusual reactions to neuroleptic (antipsychotic) medications.
Longitudinal study	A research design that involved repeated observations of the same variables over a period of time.
Mania	Behaviour that is marked by overactivity and great excitement but is also related to delusions.
Mental Health Act	Generally referring to the 1983 legislation, which allows for some people to be detained, under section 3, in a mental institution for six months.
Meta-analysis	The examination of data taken from a number of sources to attempt to show patterns or trends.
Metabolic syndrome	A cluster of conditions that affect metabolic functioning and are associated with increased fat around the waist, high blood pressure, increased blood sugar and can result in the development of type 2 diabetes, heart disease and a stroke.
Neuroleptic effect	Drugs that have a calming effect on the patient, reducing agitation and confusion.
Neuroleptic malignant syndrome (NMS)	A potentially life-threatening side effect of antipsychotics that involves stiffness, high blood pressure, increased heart rate, but can also lead to a coma.
Psychotropic drugs	Any drug that is capable of affecting the mind, emotions and behaviour.

Key word	Definition
Risperidone	An antipsychotic that binds more strongly than clozapine and reduces activity in both dopamine and serotonin.
Tardive dyskinesia	An extrapyramidal side effect of antipsychotics that is characterised by involuntary muscle movements.
Tricyclic compounds	A chemical compound that contains three interconnected rings of atoms. They are often used to treat depression but can also be used to treat other conditions.

Plenary: Exam-style questions and answers with advisory comments

Question 1.

Outline the difference between typical and atypical antipsychotics. [4 marks]

Marks for this question: AO1 = 4

Advice: In a question like this, it's important to make sure you are clearly explaining the difference, rather than just identifying/outlining what each one is. You will need to show understanding in your answer, so try to explain it in such a way that someone who knows nothing about it could understand. There is no need to provide any analysis or evaluation as all of the marks are for AO1: Knowledge and understanding.

Possible answer: Antipsychotics are divided into two types, conventional or typical antipsychotics and atypical antipsychotics. Both of them work by blocking dopamine receptors but they work in slightly different ways. Typical antipsychotics such as chlorpromazine work by blocking dopamine receptors at the synapse, and they are more long-lasting than some of the atypical antipsychotics like clozapine, which only blocks dopamine receptors temporarily. This temporary blocking leads on to another difference, which is that clozapine has fewer extrapyramidal side effects than chlorpromazine. Another difference is that atypical antipsychotics don't just work on dopamine receptors but also work on other neurotransmitters such as serotonin and glutamate. One of the issues with typical antipsychotics such as clozapine is that they are only generally effective on positive symptoms whereas other atypical antipsychotics like risperidone are effective on negative symptoms. One advantage of atypical antipsychotics is that they can be given in much smaller doses than typical antipsychotics, for example the dosage for risperidone is up to 12 mg per day, for clozapine, it is up to 300 mg per day.

Question 2.

Describe and evaluate the use of antipsychotics as a treatment for schizophrenia. [16 marks]

Marks for this question: AO1 = 6 and AO3 = 10

Advice: This question specifically focuses on the use of treatments, so it is important to explain points such as dosage and application as well as what they are. This question is looking for both skills of knowledge and understanding and analysis and evaluation. As there are 6 marks for AO1 and 10 for AO3, there should be greater emphasis on the evaluation. However, all such extended writing questions are marked holistically and therefore it is important that the knowledge is accurate and detailed and that the evaluation is clear and effective.

Possible answer: The biological approach has contributed to the treatment of schizophrenia. The most common treatment is antipsychotic medication and, as it has been well-established that levels of dopamine have a strong correlation with the disorder, it has appeared sensible to use drugs that alter these levels to treat it. Antipsychotic medication is psychotropic in that it attempts to alter the chemical balance in the body of the sufferer and hopefully lower the levels of dopamine.

The first generation of antipsychotic drugs, known as typical or conventional antipsychotics, were originally used for their neuroleptic effect, as they tended to act as a sedative and so were used to calm patients down, having been previously used as a pre-surgery drug and even in the treatment of chronic hiccups. However, in later years, these drugs became more associated with the reduction of dopamine and it was recognised that it was this that was the important factor. One of the first of these drugs to be used was chlorpromazine, which is one of a class of drugs called phenothiazines, which works as an antagonist for a number of neurotransmitter receptors, including dopamine, and leads to the reduction of the action of dopamine by blocking its receptors at the synapse. It can be taken as a tablet, syrup or injection depending on the severity and speed of action required. Most patients will be prescribed the tablet form in small doses of 50–75 mg per day initially, working up to around 400 mg per day in the long term. The drug is noted for its effectiveness in the treatment of mania symptoms that are associated with schizophrenia, particularly hallucinations. Unfortunately, these typical antipsychotics were found to have extrapyramidal side effects, such as tardive dyskinesia and, even worse, neuroleptic malignant syndrome, consequently, the need for a drug with less serious side effects was identified.

The second generation of drugs, sometimes referred to as atypical drugs because they don't have the typical side effects associated with the first-generation drugs, include clozapine and risperidone. Clozapine works in a similar way to chlorpromazine by blocking dopamine receptors but does this more weakly than chlorpromazine by only temporarily blocking these receptors, which may help to explain the lack of extrapyramidal side effects. However, clozapine has also been found to have an effect on negative symptoms of schizophrenia such as avolition and apathy, as well as having an effect on mood and cognition, therefore, it seems to have an effect on other neurotransmitters, e.g. serotonin and glutamate.

Risperidone was developed in the 1990s and has a stronger action than clozapine for dopamine and serotonin receptors meaning that the drug can be used in lower doses than clozapine, typically starting with 4–8 mg per day, increasing to around 12 mg per day. Like clozapine, risperidone only binds to dopamine receptors temporarily, so that the risk of extrapyramidal side effects is low.

The problem of side effects is a major problem for all antipsychotics. There are many of them, ranging from restlessness, weight gain and sexual problems to the reduction of white blood cells and even death. Typical antipsychotics such as chlorpromazine have been particularly associated with tardive dyskinesia, which involves the patient displaying involuntary movements of the mouth, lips and jaw and, even more seriously, neuroleptic malignant syndrome, which involves a very high fever, accelerated heart rate and autonomic nervous system dysfunction as well as death. It seems as though typical antipsychotics block dopamine activity in the hypothalamus, which affects autonomic function and leads to problems in a number of areas of normal functioning. Even though atypical antipsychotics have been found to have fewer serious side effects, it is still the case that what may seem to be less serious for some could be enough to put other people off taking the drugs and deciding that they are better off with schizophrenia than with the problems related to weight gain and sexual dysfunction. Furthermore, there have been many reported cases of suicide while on these drugs, although Pompili et al. have shown that antipsychotics and, in particular clozapine, have significant anti-suicidal properties. This suggests that it isn't easy for psychiatrists to decide on what may be the most appropriate drugs and, in recent times, there has been a resurgence of the use of clozapine, as many regard it as more effective than the more modern drugs.

With regard to effectiveness, a meta-analysis by Leucht et al. involving over 28,000 patients, mostly with chronic versions of schizophrenia, was able to show that compared to 30 per cent of the placebo control group, 51 per cent of the antipsychotic medicated group had at least a minimal response and 23 per cent had a good response compared with 14 per cent in the control group. Other research by Leucht et al. has shown that relapse rates are significantly improved in those taking antipsychotic medication compared to a placebo control group with 27 per cent of the medicated group suffering a relapse, compared to 64 per cent of the placebo group. However, in a *longitudinal study* looking into the use of antipsychotic medication over 20 years, Harrow et al. found that while the drugs were effective in the short term, in the long term they were actually leading to a prolonging of psychotic symptoms when compared with a control group who did not use the drugs in the long term. This suggests that the prolonged use of antipsychotic medication may actually be detrimental and that patients with schizophrenia would be better off not taking it. This may be because the effect of blocking dopamine receptors may be compensated for by the brain increasing the number or density of dopamine receptors and possibly creating supersensitivity to dopamine in the person receiving the antipsychotics, which can then lead to more serious side effects and decrease the effectiveness.

Further problems with the use of antipsychotics have led some to argue that far from making the brain better, antipsychotics are actually damaging the brain. According to Lawrie (2018), it has become clear over the last 20 years that schizophrenia is associated with significant reduction in brain volume for both grey and white matter. Lawrie provided a review of a number of studies that looked into this effect and considered whether it was the disorder that was causing this or the use of antipsychotics. These problems have led to the criticism that the prolonged use of antipsychotics can create a problem of 'zombification' and that perhaps the drugs are simply being used as a chemical straitjacket to control those with schizophrenia, rather than as a beneficial form of treatment.

References

Adams, C.E., Awad, G.A., Rathbone, J., Thornley, B. and Soares-Weiser, K. (2014) Chlorpromazine versus placebo for schizophrenia. *Cochrane Database of Systematic Reviews*, (1).

Bagnall, A.M., Jones, L., Ginnelly, L., Lewis, R., Glanville, J., Gilbody, S., Davies, L., Torgerson, D. and Kleijnen, J. (2003) A systematic review of atypical antipsychotic drugs in schizophrenia. In *NIHR Health Technology Assessment Programme: Executive Summaries*. NIHR Journals Library, National Institute for Health Research. Available from: https://www.ncbi.nlm.nih.gov/books/NBK62258.

General Medical Council (GMC) (1998) *Seeking patients' consent: The ethical considerations*. London: GMC.

Gautam, S. and Meena, P.S. (2011) Drug-emergent metabolic syndrome in patients with schizophrenia receiving atypical (second-generation) antipsychotics. *Indian Journal of Psychiatry*, 53 (2): 128.

Green, A.I. and Brown, E.S. (2006) Comorbid schizophrenia and substance abuse. *The Journal of Clinical Psychiatry*, 67 (9): e08–e08.

Harrow, M., Jobe, T.H. and Faull, R.N. (2014). Does treatment of schizophrenia with antipsychotic medications eliminate or reduce psychosis? A 20-year multi-follow-up study. *Psychological Medicine*, 44 (14): 3007–3016.

Kapur, S. and Remington, G. (2001) Atypical antipsychotics: New directions and new challenges in the treatment of schizophrenia. *Annual Review of Medicine*, 52 (1): 503–517.

Kesby, J.P., Eyles, D.W., McGrath, J.J. and Scott, J.G. (2018) Dopamine, psychosis and schizophrenia: The widening gap between basic and clinical neuroscience. *Translational Psychiatry*, 8 (1): 1–12.

Lawrie S.M. (2018) Are structural brain changes in schizophrenia related to antipsychotic medication? A narrative review of the evidence from a clinical perspective. *Therapeutic Advances in Psychopharmacology*, 8 (11): 319–326.

Leucht, S., Tardy, M., Komossa, K., Heres, S., Kissling, W., Salanti, G. and Davis, J.M. (2012) Antipsychotic drugs versus placebo for relapse prevention in schizophrenia: A systematic review and meta-analysis. *The Lancet*, 379 (9831): 2063–2071.

Leucht, S., Chaimani, A., Leucht, C., Huhn, M., Mavridis, D., Helfer, B., Samara, M., Cipriani, A., Geddes, J.R., Salanti, G. and Davis, J.M. (2018)

60 years of placebo-controlled antipsychotic drug trials in acute schizophrenia: Meta-regression of predictors of placebo response. *Schizophrenia Research*, 201: 315–323.

Marder, S.R. and Meibach, R.C. (1994) Risperidone in the treatment of schizophrenia. *The American Journal of Psychiatry*, 151 (6): 825.

Martin, L. Nursing homes turning residents into 'zombies', Aged Care Royal Commission to hear. *The Guardian*, 15 January 2019.

Moncrieff, J. (2013). *The Bitterest Pills: The Troubling Story of Antipsychotic Drugs.* London: Springer.

Pompili, M., Baldessarini, R.J., Forte, A., Erbuto, D., Serafini, G., Fiorillo, A., Amore, M. and Girardi, P. (2016) Do atypical antipsychotics have anti-suicidal effects? A hypothesis-generating overview. *International Journal of Molecular Sciences*, 17 (10): 1700.

PS, R (On the Application Of) V Responsible Medical Officer and Anor, England and Wales High Court (Administrative Court), 10 October 2003.

Ramachandraiah, C.T., Subramaniam, N. and Tancer, M. (2009) The story of antipsychotics: Past and present. *Indian Journal of Psychiatry*, 51 (4): 324.

Chapter 6
Psychological therapies for schizophrenia

Cognitive behaviour therapy and family therapy as used in the treatment of schizophrenia. Token economies as used in the management of schizophrenia.

AO1 (Knowledge and understanding): What are the psychological therapies for schizophrenia?

Psychological approaches to treating schizophrenia

In Chapter 4, consideration was given to the influence of psychological factors on schizophrenia and the possibility that there were both environmental and cognitive factors causing the symptoms of the disorder. The role of the family was looked at as a risk factor for schizophrenia and also as playing a part in the relapse of those suffering with schizophrenia; additionally the role of cognitive dysfunction was considered as a potential cause of the symptoms of schizophrenia.

In this chapter, these factors will be revisited with a consideration of how the effect of both of them could be reduced through the use of psychological techniques aimed directly at dealing with dysfunctions in cognition and family communication. We will also look at the use of token economies in the management of schizophrenia, which can make it possible for those suffering with schizophrenia to have more favourable outcomes both inside and outside institutions.

The role of cognitive behaviour therapy in treating schizophrenia

If we believe that cognitive dysfunction is the cause of the symptoms of schizophrenia and that dysfunction in thought processes is contributing to disturbances in a person's ability to make sense of the world, then it would seem logical to try to change that perception using a treatment that could make dysfunctional thought processes functional and adaptive.

Cognitive behaviour therapy (CBT) is a treatment that is designed to change both cognition, our understanding/perception of the world around us, and behaviour, how we respond to stimuli that might challenge our understanding/perception of the world around us. The belief is that if we can change the dysfunctional thoughts that are causing confusing and irrational beliefs in the mind of the person with schizophrenia, then we can change the maladaptive behaviour that arises from these thoughts and hopefully allow the person to cope with challenging stimuli such as delusions and hallucinations in their everyday life.

Beck and Rector (2000) suggest that the focus of cognitive behaviour therapy is on the notion that the psychosis has developed in a situation that is unique to the patient – this is crucial to establishing a trusting relationship between therapist and patient. Although, the situation is more challenging than working with a depressed patient, the same kind of techniques should be used, e.g. gentle questioning and empirical testing of beliefs.

Techniques used in CBT for schizophrenia

1. The therapist develops a trusting and collaborative relationship with the patient.
2. The patient is given time to explain their experiences, e.g. voices, delusions, etc.
3. The therapist works with the patient to identify situational or emotional triggers that activate these experiences.
4. The therapist can use reality testing on the patient's beliefs with techniques such as:
   * Socratic questioning: Can others hear the voices? Why not?
   * Focusing: For example, the patient can focus on the characteristics of imagined attackers and create criteria that would help someone else to identify them as attackers, e.g. an aggressive stance. The more they focus on the imagined attackers, the more they realise that they don't fit the criteria.
5. Homework is used to encourage the patient to create experiments to test out their beliefs and to develop strategies to deal with them as well as encouraging activity schedules involving pleasurable tasks.

Each session should last between 15 and 45 minutes and should be as flexible as possible with frequent breaks and the opportunity to change the focus of the session.

> **Think!**
>
> How would you use these techniques to deal with the negative symptoms of schizophrenia?
>
> Is it the same as the way you would treat the positive symptoms?

The role of family therapy in treating schizophrenia

In Chapter 4, close consideration was given to the role of the family in creating the conditions in which relapse was likely due to the communication problems that can be a feature of all families. Consequently, family therapy looks not only at treating the individual suffering with schizophrenia but also at working with the family to try to ensure that the communication patterns that could lead to relapse aren't present but are replaced with more positive patterns of communication that can lead to more positive outcomes for both the individual and the family.

Pharoah et al. (2010) suggest that the specific aim of family therapy is to reduce the levels of expressed emotion and stress, alongside enabling the relatives of the patient to deal with any problems that may occur, in order to prevent relapse and the need for further hospitalisation.

Specific interventions

1. Involving all family members in the therapeutic process to ensure harmony and consistency.
2. Reducing the burden of caring for the person by lowering the feeling of stress in the family.
3. Encouraging the belief that family members can anticipate and solve problems.
4. Lowering the levels of guilt and anger expressed by the family.
5. The setting of realistic goals for patient performance and encouraging family members to have a balance between caring for the patient and having time for themselves.

Think!

How do you think the family might react to the interventions outlined above?
Do you think it would be easy to get everyone on board with this?

Token economies

Managing the behaviour of patients with schizophrenia can be very challenging and can be a particular problem with regard to the negative symptoms of schizophrenia, as the patient may display maladaptive behaviour such as poor hygiene and being unwilling to engage in social/therapeutic activities. This is likely to be a particular problem for those who have spent considerable time in a mental institution, making it difficult for them to cope on their own in the outside world or to live with relatives.

Token economies started being used in the 1960s and were used extensively throughout the 1970s. Although their use has declined since then, they are still used in some form today. A token economy programme is based on the theory of operant conditioning, which involves the use of positive reinforcement. It is intended to identify the behaviour that is undesirable and the reinforcers that maintain such behaviour and then to change the environment so that those reinforcers are removed. It also aims to identify the desirable behaviour and provide rewards in the form of tokens that are worthless in themselves, e.g. pieces of coloured card, but that can be exchanged for the things the patient desires such as coffee or TV time.

The hope is that the use of secondary reinforcers in this way will modify the behaviour of the patient so that their behaviour can be more easily managed by those involved in the care of the patient both inside and outside the mental institution. This behaviour modification is not intended as a form of cure or even treatment for their disorder but may make it more likely that they can live outside the institution and may even be beneficial in encouraging them to take their medication or become involved in therapeutic activities. One of the problems facing people who have spent time in a mental institution is that they can become institutionalised, making it difficult for them to adjust to living outside the institution. The hope is that using token economies can help them be ready to face the challenges of daily life, e.g. cooking, cleaning, being on time for work, etc.

Question time

What is CBT attempting to challenge in the mind of a person with schizophrenia?

Is family therapy attempting to deal with the cause of schizophrenia? If not, what is it attempting to deal with?

How do token economies help the person with schizophrenia?

Mini plenary

Identify the stages in treating/managing behaviour used by each of the three methods below:

CBT	Family therapy	Token economy

AO2 (Application of knowledge): How does this apply in practice?

Interleave me now

Operant conditioning

B.F. Skinner (1965 [1953]) believed that it wasn't necessary to try to look into the mind in order to understand human behaviour, but instead we can focus on the observable actions of people as they operate on their environment. Learning is part of a process of trial and error in which we operate in our environment. If the outcome is pleasant or satisfying then we are more likely to repeat it in that same situation. This idea was developed from the work of E.L. Thorndike (1905) (from his work with cats attempting to escape from a puzzle box) and developed later by Skinner with the use of the 'Skinner box' where rats received a reward for pressing a lever.

Skinner became interested in learning through the association between a response and its consequences and was particularly interested in the role of positive reinforcement in learning. This is a positive consequence or reward that occurs directly after the behaviour and is therefore associated with it. Skinner believed that this process could be used to modify human behaviour.

Behaviour modification and the token economy

Skinner's theory involved the use of reinforcers to change behaviour. In the Skinner box, a rat would receive food for pressing the lever, which would encourage it to press the lever again the next time it was hungry. Food was therefore being used as a primary reinforcer as it satisfied a physical need such as hunger. Some reinforcers don't fulfil a physical need but do become associated with physical needs and are therefore referred to as secondary reinforcers. An obvious secondary reinforcer for a human would be money, as we are aware that it can give us access to primary reinforcers and it is, therefore, rewarding. However, there are other forms of secondary reinforcers that have similar associations, and these are used extensively by parents, teachers and others working in institutional settings, e.g. prisons, mental institutions, etc.

Secondary reinforcers are nothing more than a token that can be exchanged for something desirable, e.g. paper money has no value in itself (it's just paper) but we are aware that it can be exchanged for something that satisfies our physical needs and is therefore reinforcing. Similar tokens are used in schools by teachers to encourage appropriate behaviour in their students, by parents to encourage children to do the right thing at home, and by prison officers and therapists to encourage desirable behaviour within institutions.

Think!

What kinds of secondary reinforcers are used in schools?

Do these secondary reinforcers work? If not, why not?

Interleave me now

Cultural bias

The issue of cultural bias is something that occurs with alarming regularity in various areas of psychological research. It can cause problems of misunderstanding and sometimes even discrimination. We have seen previously that cultural bias can be seen when taking a universal approach to research, whereas, if we want to prevent bias, we should consider a more relativist approach.

Universality would suggest that it is possible to apply the findings of psychological research to everyone regardless of their apparent differences.

Cultural relativism involves accepting that norms and values are different and that it's not possible to create a universal set of laws or rules that apply to everyone regardless of culture.

We have already seen in this book how cultural bias can cause problems of diagnosis, but it may also be that it can cause problems in treatment, particularly when those treatments involve psychosocial elements that may need a greater recognition of the relative differences between cultural groups.

Cultural bias in therapy

Benish et al. (2011) argued that it is important to recognise that psychotherapy isn't something that exists in a void without social and cultural context, but it is very clearly created in situations that have a clear dominant majority culture and one or more ethnic minority cultures. In this situation, psychotherapy is created by those within the dominant majority culture who may then apply it to the ethnic minority cultures without proper regard for the cultural differences.

If we attempt to take a universal approach to this and argue that a therapy should work for everyone, we are potentially setting ourselves up for failure, as we fail to take into account cultural relativism and the need for an approach that is created by and for those within these ethnic minorities. This is particularly true when we are looking at therapies that are created within Western Europe and North America, as these places are likely to have within them ethnic minority cultures from many places around the world.

Benish et al. wanted to look at the use of 'unadapted psychotherapy', based around the idea that the same methods can be used for all groups, and therefore based on a universal view of mental illness in which the causes and therefore treatments are the same. They then wanted to compare the effectiveness of using this with ethnic minority groups (African-American, Asian-American, Puerto Rico Latino/Hispanic and non-Puerto Rico Latino/Hispanic) with 'adapted' psychotherapy where the session had been prepared based on the specific characteristics of the ethnic group. Some of the adaptations included conducting the session in the client's native language and matching the ethnicity of the therapist with that of the client.

They found that culturally adapted therapy was significantly more effective than unadapted therapy for use with the ethnic minority groups identified above. This suggests that unadapted therapy, which is generally practised throughout psychotherapy sessions, may involve considerable cultural bias and therefore mean that it is not fit for purpose with those groups who are not a part of the dominant, majority culture.

Question time

What does this tell us about the use of psychotherapy with people from different cultures?

How would unadapted therapy need to be changed to make it useful for different cultures?

Why might this be difficult to do?

Aggie has spent the last year in a mental institution being treated for her diagnosis of schizophrenia and is now due for release. However, the staff are concerned that she isn't ready to face the challenges of life outside of the institution.

Explain how the staff might use a token economy to help Aggie be better prepared for life outside of the institution.

AO3 (Analysis and evaluation of knowledge): How useful are these therapies?

Are there fewer ethical issues with psychological therapies?

One of the problems identified with the use of drugs has been that they have sometimes been regarded as chemical straitjackets that are simply used to constrain and control those with schizophrenia, just as the straitjacket used to be used in days gone by. This raises questions of ethics that may not be applicable to psychological therapies, as they have fewer problems with consent and with physical and psychological side effects. This should mean that psychological therapies are significantly safer and less likely to infringe on human rights than the biological treatments.

CBT, as put forward by Beck and Rector (2000), takes an individualistic approach to treatment, recognising as it does that the experience of each individual is unique and that there are specific circumstances that have led to the development of schizophrenia. Furthermore, in attempting to create a trusting and cooperative relationship with the patient, it appears to be recognising the need for a consensual approach, which is less likely to cause stress.

Family therapy also appears to have fewer ethical issues as the approach is also one of collaboration with family members and the need to create an alliance that should be seen as respectful of the needs of all individuals within the family. There may be the potential for some blame to be felt by the family as the therapy is based on the view that further problems experienced by the patient might be caused by the behaviour of family members towards that person, which could lead to feelings of guilt. However, the approach put forward by Pharoah et al. (2010) was concerned to emphasise the need to avoid feelings of guilt among family members.

Unfortunately, there have been ethical issues raised in relation to token economies, particularly in relation to the possibility of withdrawing, or at least holding back, things that might be regarded as a human right in most circumstances. The fact that certain items come to be regarded as a privilege, e.g. coffee/TV time, might be questioned by some as these are not exactly luxuries. It is also possible that the experience of being involved in such schemes is humiliating for the individuals involved as they may feel like they are being treated like children, particularly as their use with children is so common.

This suggests that although psychological therapies may be able to reduce some of the ethical issues raised when treating those with schizophrenia, particularly in relation to consent and the possibility of harm, they may still raise questions of human rights, if the patients involved in these treatments are not afforded the same rights and privileges that others enjoy – particularly if we accept that those with schizophrenia carry no blame for their disorder.

Think!

Do you think these ethical issues are better or worse than those raised with the use of biological treatments?

Does the fact that these treatments are likely to be used alongside drugs raise more objections?

Is it right to make patients feel more responsible for their own recovery?

One of the criticisms that is often levelled against biological treatments and, in particular, the use of drugs, is that they take away all responsibility from the patient for their own recovery. Giving someone a drug and suggesting that it will sort them out may make the patient feel that they don't have to do anything to help themselves.

However, psychological therapies don't do that. They will try to make the patient, and sometimes their families, take more responsibility for their recovery by trying to involve them in activities that could lead to the reduction of their symptoms, reduction of the possibility that they will need to return to hospital, or an increase in their ability to function normally outside an institution or possibly even be able to take up employment.

As shown above, it can often be quite challenging to get the patient to confront their own irrational thoughts and to undertake reality testing experiments, in order to help them see the lack of logic in their thoughts and behaviour. Family therapy places quite a lot of responsibility on the family to change their approach to caring for a relative with schizophrenia by altering their own thoughts, feelings and behaviour towards the patient, either on their own or often through training sessions used by the therapist. Token economy requires the patient to change their own behaviour through forms of reinforcement designed to get them to behave in ways that others regard as more socially acceptable.

This level of responsibility can be regarded as positive as it makes the patient and their family more proactive in their recovery and hopefully creates the possibility of employing these forms of behaviour in the future without the need for any further intervention by health and care services. In that sense it fits very well with the current emphasis in the NHS and social care services on empowering patients.

However, it could be that it places too much responsibility on people who are already finding it very difficult to cope and for whom the extra level of pressure could lead to their problem becoming much worse. Consequently, it is a difficult road to tread and may require significant training, both for those delivering the treatment and for those on the receiving end.

Are psychological therapies effective?

The effectiveness of psychological therapies for the treatment of schizophrenia is likely to be hampered by the lack of insight shown by sufferers, and this is nowhere more true than in the use of CBT. Cognitive therapies require a certain level of insight into the disorder in order to change the thinking of the patient. However, there have been some meta-analyses that have suggested some limited effectiveness for the therapy.

Hofman et al. (2012), conducted a review of meta-analyses into the use of CBT for schizophrenia and other psychotic disorders and found that there was evidence of a beneficial effect on positive symptoms, hallucinations and delusions but also found evidence suggesting a small effect on negative symptoms as well as a beneficial effect on other outcomes that were not the direct target of the treatment, e.g. general functioning and social anxiety. However, they found little effect on relapse or hospitalisation, particularly when compared to family therapy.

Family therapy itself has been the focus of meta-analyses and Pharoah et al. (2010) conducted one such study to look at the effect of the therapy on relapse and hospitalisation rates. In a review of over 50 trials, they found that family therapy may reduce the frequency of relapse and hospital admission but also improve compliance with medication and improve the level of expressed emotion in the family. A further meta-analysis by Bird et al. (2010) compared family therapy to CBT and found that while CBT reduced the severity of symptoms, only family therapy had an effect on reducing relapse and hospital admission rates.

In relation to token economies, there is less evidence due to the fact that it isn't used in such a systematic way as some of the other therapies. McMonagle and Sultana (2000), conducted a small meta-analysis of just three trials using token economies and found a small effect on negative symptoms, providing some support for the approach, but they questioned whether such results could be reproduced in other cases.

Is it possible to use psychological therapies without the use of drugs?

One of the question marks hanging over the use of psychological therapies is whether they are actually an alternative to biological treatments or whether they are just complementary to the use of drugs and can only be used alongside them. It is often the case that therapies such as CBT can only be useful if the patient is already in a sufficiently calm state brought on by the use of antipsychotics.

Morrison et al. (2018) randomly assigned 75 patients suffering with psychosis to a CBT-only group (26), an antipsychotics-only group (24) and a CBT-plus-antipsychotics group (25). They found significantly greater improvement for the CBT-plus-antipsychotics group than for the CBT-only group but also found no significant difference between the CBT-plus-antipsychotics group and the antipsychotics-only group. This suggests that it may be the antipsychotics that are making the crucial difference between success and failure in these treatments and that while CBT may be helpful, it isn't making a significant difference to the outcomes of the patients, certainly not without the use of drugs. However, they did also find that there were fewer adverse side effects in the CBT-only group than the other two, although this isn't exactly surprising.

Many studies have found better relapse and hospitalisation results when using family therapy as opposed to using drug treatment alone, e.g. Xiong et al. (1994), however these studies have generally all been conducted using a comparison of family therapy plus drugs with just drugs alone. The findings of such studies are that there are significantly better results using a combined approach. However, in a review of such studies Barbato and D'Avanzo (2000) suggested that it wasn't possible to use family therapy without the use of medication and that the use of medication was uncontrolled in most of these studies (including in Xiong et al., 1994) and therefore it may be that success in these studies was due to better use of drugs rather than the use of family therapy.

All this suggests that the successful use of any other form of therapy relies on it being used in combination with drugs and may even point to the idea that drugs alone can be the most effective treatment for schizophrenia and other psychotic disorders.

Question time

What are the alternatives to the psychological therapies outlined in this chapter? Are these alternatives likely to be enough on their own to treat schizophrenia? Are these alternatives better or worse than psychological therapies? Can they be seen as complementary?

Mini plenary

Using the evaluation points above, try to identify arguments for and against psychological therapies in the treatment of schizophrenia.

Arguments for	Arguments against

A modern issue: is the use of psychological therapies cost-effective?

A constant issue with the use of any treatment is cost and this is particularly so in the UK, due to the fact that the costs need to be met by an increasingly expensive National Health Service. Whether or not we can afford psychological therapies isn't just a case of whether we can afford to provide the services as well as the cost of drugs. It is also a case of whether these services will lead to financial benefits in terms of allowing people to be treated without the need for institutionalisation and for society as a whole in the form of increased employability for those being treated.

New research

COSTING STATEMENT

Psychosis and schizophrenia in adults: Treatment and management implementing the NICE guideline on psychosis and schizophrenia in adults (CG178)

Published: February 2014

A NICE report published in 2014 identified that the cost of treating the 220,000 patients with schizophrenia in England and Wales in 2007 accounted for 30 per cent of the total expenditure for adult mental health and social care services. The costs of the service in England in 2007 were believed to be in the region of £2.2 billion and are expected to rise to £3.7 billion in 2026. However, this figure is only focused on the costs of the service and doesn't take account of the cost of lost employment, which is known to be a major issue with patients suffering from psychosis, particularly those treated without the use of psychological therapies in the early stages of the disorder. With the cost of lost employment included, the total figure was estimated to be roughly double that figure.

Consequently, the report recommends that the use of early intervention therapies was very important for the treatment of schizophrenia and psychosis and that if early intervention strategies were put into place, particularly those involving the use of CBT then there could be significant savings in the long term even though this would lead to extra costs in the short term. The estimated figures from NICE show that if early intervention strategies had been provided for 60 per cent of new cases of schizophrenia in 2010, savings could have been in the region of £9 million per year and that if the services were rolled out to include 100 per cent coverage by 2026 then savings to the NHS could be in the region of £18.4 million per year.

This costing was further reinforced by unpublished data from the Institute of Psychiatry, which estimated that although the cost of an early intervention service would be £813 per person in the first year, the savings in the following year could be as much as £1,803.

The conclusion of the report was that this long-term approach may be beneficial but that the costing would need to be considered at a local level as there is considerable variation in the services provided locally and some areas may need greater investment than others.

Question time

What does this article tell us about the cost effectiveness of treatments for schizophrenia?

Why might those in charge of the NHS and particularly the government, be unwilling to implement such a service?

Why is there local variation in the services currently provided by the National Health Service?

1. What are the psychological approaches to treating schizophrenia based on?
2. What is the role of CBT in treating schizophrenia?
3. What techniques are used in CBT?
4. What is the role of family therapy in treating schizophrenia?
5. What specific interventions are involved in family therapy?
6. What is the role of token economies in managing schizophrenia?
7. How does operant conditioning relate to the use of token economies?
8. How is behaviour modification related to the use of token economies in the management of schizophrenia?
9. Why is there cultural bias in therapy?
10. Are there fewer ethical issues with psychological therapies?
11. Is it right to make patients feel more responsible for their own recovery?
12. Are psychological therapies effective?
13. Is it possible to use psychological therapies without the use of drugs?
14. Is the use of psychological therapies cost-effective?

Glossary

Key word	Definition
Behaviour modification	An approach to therapy that uses positive and negative reinforcement to change behaviour.
Chemical straitjackets	A term used to compare the use of antipsychotics to the use of a jacket that was used as a restraint in mental institutions and had the effect of controlling the patient without having any other benefit.
Cognitive behaviour therapy (CBT)	A talking therapy that is focused on changing the dysfunctional thoughts and behaviour of the client by challenging their thoughts and encouraging them to test out their thoughts in real-life behaviour settings.
Cultural relativism	The recognition that different cultures have different norms and values and no attempt should be made to apply universal values to them.
Culturally adapted therapy	Changing the therapy so that it can be applied to people from different cultures, e.g. providing a therapist who speaks the same language.
Focusing	A technique used in CBT that attempts to identify the detail in someone's beliefs.
Homework	The behavioural part of CBT that encourages patients to practise the strategies they have learned in the session.

Key word	Definition
Institutionalised	Becoming so used to being part of an institution that you find it hard to leave.
Meta-analyses	The examination of data taken from a number of sources to attempt to show patterns or trends.
NICE	The National Institute for Health and Care Excellence is an independent organisation set up by the government to make decisions about the appropriate use of health and care for the whole population, including those with mental health problems.
Operant conditioning	A method of learning that works through providing positive and negative reinforcement for behaviour.
Positive reinforcement	The use of rewards to change someone's behaviour.
Primary reinforcer	A reward that satisfies a basic human need such as hunger.
Reality testing	A technique used in CBT that involves challenging the beliefs of the patient to try to get them to recognise that they don't fit with reality.
Secondary reinforcers	Things that can be exchanged for primary reinforcers, e.g. money.
Skinner box	A piece of apparatus used by B.F. Skinner in his work with rats that could isolate the animal and control its access to rewards, e.g. pressing a lever to get food.
Socratic questioning	A form of questioning that tries to find out the underlying assumptions in someone's beliefs.
Unadapted psychotherapy	Applying the same form of therapy to everyone regardless of their individual differences.
Universality	The possibility of applying the findings of psychological research to everyone regardless of their apparent differences.

Plenary: Exam-style questions and answers with advisory comments

Question 1.

Outline the use of CBT in the treatment of schizophrenia. [4 marks]

Marks for this question: AO1 = 4

Advice: In a question like this, it's important to make sure you are clearly explaining the techniques used, rather than just identifying/outlining what CBT is. The best way to approach this is to refer to the different stages involved in the use of CBT. There is no need to provide any analysis or evaluation as all of the marks are for AO1: Knowledge and understanding.

Possible answer: CBT involves a number of stages that are generally used to help the patient come to a better understanding and to be able to cope with their disorder.

First, the therapist will try to develop a trusting and collaborative relationship with the patient. Then they will give the patient time to explain their experiences and what is causing them a problem. The therapist will work with the patient to try to identify the triggers that activate their experiences. Then they will use reality testing techniques such as Socratic questioning to try to get the patient to recognise that their experiences aren't real, e.g. why can't other people hear the voices? Finally, they will set homework to encourage the patient to use the strategies they have learned in real life situations, so that they can cope better in their daily lives.

Question 2.

Schizophrenia is a disorder that is characterised by a separation from reality such that sufferers experience hallucinations and delusions that have no basis in reality. Auditory hallucinations will sometimes involve negative comments made by a voice that only they can hear, suggesting that the sufferer isn't capable of performing certain tasks or jobs. These symptoms can cause major problems for the families of sufferers as they try to care for and cope with someone in their house who needs a lot of care but isn't always easy to communicate with. Families will sometimes feel that it is too much and feel the need for the person to be treated in an institution or hospital.

With reference to the section above, discuss the use of CBT and family therapy in the treatment of schizophrenia. [16 marks]

Marks for this question: AO1 = 6, AO2 = 4 and AO3 = 6

Advice: This question is looking for all three skills of: knowledge and understanding; application of knowledge; and analysis and evaluation. As there are 6 marks for AO1 and 6 for AO3, there should be a roughly equal emphasis on knowledge and understanding and evaluation. However, with 4 marks for AO2 in this question, there is also the need for significant reference to the material in the stem. It's important to ensure that you have shown the examiner that you have applied your knowledge to the stem, so it's always a good idea to use some of the words/sentences/phrases from the stem.

Possible answer: CBT is a therapy used in the treatment of schizophrenia that is based on the belief that if we can change the dysfunctional thoughts that are causing confusing and irrational beliefs in the mind of the person with schizophrenia, then we can change the maladaptive behaviour that arises from these thoughts and hopefully allow the person to cope with challenging stimuli such as delusions and auditory hallucinations in their everyday life.

First, the therapist will try to develop a trusting and collaborative relationship with the patient. Then they will give the patient time to explain their experiences and what is causing them a problem. The therapist will work with the patient to try to identify the triggers that activate their experiences. Then they will use reality testing techniques such as Socratic questioning to try to get the patient to recognise that their experiences, such as auditory hallucinations, aren't real, e.g. why can't other people hear the voices? Finally, they will set homework to encourage the patient to use the strategies they have learned in real life situations. This will also involve reality testing, as the patient is encouraged to become involved in tasks and activities that are pleasurable and that may serve to challenge the 'negative comments' being made. This should lead to the patient possibly recognising that such comments are coming from within themselves and are due to their own fears rather than the voice of someone else.

Family therapy looks not only at treating the individual who is suffering with schizophrenia but also at working with the family to try to ensure that the communication problems referred to in the source, which could also lead to relapse, aren't present but are replaced with more positive patterns of communication that can lead to better outcomes for both the individual and the family.

Pharoah et al. suggest that the specific aim of family therapy is to reduce the levels of expressed emotion and stress, alongside enabling the relatives of the patient to deal with any problems that may occur, to prevent relapse and the need for the person to be treated in an institution or hospital.

Pharoah et al. identified some specific interventions that may help the family to cope, one of which is to involve all family members in the therapeutic process to ensure harmony and consistency. They believe that it is necessary to encourage the belief that they, the family, can cope in order to discourage the feeling that 'it is too much for them'. Hopefully, this will help to reduce the burden of caring for the person and lower the feeling of stress in the family. They also believe that it is important to lower the levels of guilt and anger felt by the family, as this may also be beneficial for everyone involved in the care of the patient. Finally, they suggest setting realistic goals for patient performance so that no one is surprised, or disappointed, if progress is slow. They also pointed out the need to try to encourage the family to have a balance between caring for the person with schizophrenia and having time for themselves.

One of the issues that regularly applies to the treatment of schizophrenia with biological treatments like drugs is that there can be ethical issues as the person may not consent to the treatment and the drugs can have harmful side effects. These problems should be less with psychological therapies as they are more consensual and have no obvious side effects. This is particularly true with CBT as Beck and Rector have argued that the whole focus of CBT should be on the unique nature of the disorder and, as such, the therapist should be working hard to provide a trusting relationship with the patient so that the patient is less likely to feel stressed. This should also be true of family therapy as a collaborative approach is developed so that the family and the therapist are working in partnership.

However, family therapy can cause some ethical problems as there is still the possibility that the family might feel blamed for the problems that their child is experiencing and feel guilt even though it is discouraged. Similar problems may arise in the use of CBT as a lot of responsibility is placed on the shoulders of the patient to find ways of dealing with their problem when they may be used to simply being given drugs, and having all the responsibility removed from them. This may also make the patient feel that they are in some ways to blame for their own problem and make it more difficult for them to cope.

The effectiveness of these treatments is also sometimes brought into question, particularly as they do involve extra cost compared to the use of drugs alone. However, research by Bird et al. into the use of CBT and family therapy found that CBT did reduce the severity of symptoms and family therapy had a significant impact on relapse and hospitalisation. Furthermore, research by NICE has indicated that although there may be increased cost in the short term, savings in the long term from the use of early intervention psychological therapies could be in the region of £18.4 million per year by 2026.

One further problem with the use of psychological therapies could be related to the possibility of cultural bias if we are attempting to take a universal approach and use the same unadapted therapies with all people regardless of culture. Benish et al. found that the use of culturally adapted therapy with ethnic minorities, involving the use of therapists who speak the same language and matching the ethnicity of the therapist with that of the patient, can make significant improvements in the success of the therapy and, ultimately, the more successful the therapy the greater the cost-effectiveness is likely to be, which should make us all happy.

References

Barbato, A. and D'Avanzo, B. (2000) Family interventions in schizophrenia and related disorders: A critical review of clinical trials. *Acta Psychiatrica Scandinavica*, 102 (2): 81–97.

Beck, A.T. and Rector, N.A. (2000) Cognitive therapy of schizophrenia: A new therapy for the new millennium. *American Journal of Psychotherapy*, 54 (3): 291–300.

Benish, S.G., Quintana, S. and Wampold, B.E. (2011) Culturally adapted psychotherapy and the legitimacy of myth: A direct-comparison meta-analysis. *Journal of Counseling Psychology*, 58 (3): 279.

Bird, V., Premkumar, P., Kendall, T., Whittington, C., Mitchell, J. and Kuipers, E. (2010) Early intervention services, cognitive–behavioural therapy and family intervention in early psychosis: Systematic review. *The British Journal of Psychiatry*, 197 (5): 350–356.

Hofmann, S.G., Asnaani, A., Vonk, I.J., Sawyer, A.T. and Fang, A. (2012) The efficacy of cognitive behavioral therapy: A review of meta-analyses. *Cognitive Therapy and Research*, 36 (5): 427–440.

McMonagle, T. and Sultana, A. (2000) Token economy for schizophrenia. *Cochrane Database of Systematic Reviews*, (3), Issue 3, Art. No. CD001473.

Morrison, A.P., Law, H., Carter, L., Sellers, R., Emsley, R., Pyle, M., French, P., Shiers, D., Yung, A.R., Murphy, E.K. and Holden, N. (2018) Antipsychotic drugs versus cognitive behavioural therapy versus a combination of both in people with psychosis: A randomised controlled pilot and feasibility study. *The Lancet Psychiatry*, 5 (5): 411–423.

NICE (2014) Costing statement: Psychosis and schizophrenia in adults: Treatment and management Implementing the NICE guideline on psychosis and schizophrenia in adults (CG178). Published: February 2014.

Pharoah, F., Mari, J.J., Rathbone, J. and Wong, W. (2010) Family intervention for schizophrenia. *Cochrane Database of Systematic Reviews*, Issue 12, Art. No. CD000088.

Skinner, B.F. (1965 [1953]) *Science and Human Behavior*. New York: Simon & Schuster. (Originally published by Macmillan.)

Thorndike, E. L. (1905) *The Elements of Psychology*. New York: Seiler.

Xiong, W., Phillips, M.R., Hu, X., Wang, R., Dai, Q., Kleinman, J. and Kleinman, A. (1994) Family-based intervention for schizophrenic patients in China: A randomised controlled trial. *The British Journal of Psychiatry*, 165 (2): 239–247.

Chapter 7
Interactionist approach to schizophrenia

Spec check

The importance of an interactionist approach in explaining and treating schizophrenia; the diathesis–stress model.

AO1 (Knowledge and understanding): What is an interactionist approach?

In Chapter 3, we considered the mind–body debate, which looks at whether the mind and body are the same thing and whether it is possible for one or the other to influence our behaviour. Interactionism goes beyond this debate and suggests that not only do they both exist but they both have an equal influence on our behaviour. An interactionist approach is one that says that there are two (or more) influences on our behaviour and therefore we no longer need to argue about whether schizophrenia is caused by biological factors or psychological factors because, according to this approach, it's caused by both!

> **Think!**
>
> What are the biological factors involved in schizophrenia?
> What are the psychological factors?

The diathesis–stress model explained

In the nature–nurture debate, the question wasn't whether it's nature or nurture that causes people to behave in the way that they do, it was about the relative importance of each. Consequently, there was already an acknowledgement that it isn't possible to separate nature and nurture from each other, due to the fact that both inevitably exert some kind of influence. It's virtually impossible to say that one is responsible for this and the other is responsible for that. We have already seen how hard it is to show cause and effect in the study of schizophrenia, as we can't show, for example, whether it was high levels of dopamine in a person that led to the development of schizophrenia or the other way round.

This model works in the same way with regard to schizophrenia by identifying two (or more) factors that need to work together to lead to the development of the disorder. Diathesis refers to the idea that there is a vulnerability; and stress (in this context) refers to the idea of a negative event. So the idea is that it requires both the vulnerability to be present and the negative event or environmental stressor to occur to lead someone to develop schizophrenia. One without the other would be relatively harmless but with both there is the likelihood that a person will develop schizophrenia.

Although this idea has been around for a long time, Meehl (1962) applied the idea to schizophrenia and argued that schizophrenia is essentially a genetic disorder. This led to the idea of a schizotypic personality that carried with it the idea that such a personality type was more vulnerable to stressful experiences. He continued to believe that the influence of environmental stressors was required in order for the disorder to develop in individuals with this genetic vulnerability. For Meehl, the most significant environmental influence was the type of parenting provided and in particular the behaviour of the schizophrenogenic mother.

A changing view of diathesis

Diathesis is the notion that there is something that creates a vulnerability to the development of schizophrenia. Although the original version of this was that it was genetics that created this vulnerability, modern research has suggested more of a biosocial model in which other psychological and social factors can create a predisposition to the development of schizophrenia. Essentially, it could be traumatic experiences in childhood that have created a vulnerability to schizophrenia, largely through altering the developing brain of the child and leading to other abnormalities, which we later see in the brains of those with schizophrenia. This traumagenic model of schizophrenia (Read et al., 2001) encompasses the idea that it is the trauma that is the diathesis – as it is this that makes a person more vulnerable to stress.

A changing view of stress

The original Meehl theory suggested that the most likely stressful factor to influence the development of schizophrenia was the presence of a schizophrenogenic mother. This has now become a somewhat outdated explanation, and it is most definitely not the only factor that could create the stress side of the diathesis–stress explanation. Indeed, it is now suggested that it might not be a psychological factor at all, but that it could be something more biosocial, e.g. cannabis. There is plenty of evidence cited in the previous chapters to suggest that cannabis has a role to play in the development of psychotic disorders, so it might be that the introduction of a drug that alters our biochemistry could act as the catalyst for the development of schizophrenia, rather than the drug creating the predisposing vulnerability. Houston et al. (2007) have suggested that there may be an interaction of factors with cannabis playing a significant role alongside childhood sexual abuse. They argue that, on their own, neither of these two factors was enough to trigger schizophrenia, but taken together they produced a statistically significant effect.

A neural diathesis–stress model of schizophrenia

In 1997, Walker and Diforio proposed the neural diathesis–stress model of schizophrenia, which attempted to provide a clearer explanation for what it is that creates a vulnerability to schizophrenia. Rather than just making the point that there is a genetic vulnerability, what Walker and Diforio did was to identify the specific effect that the gene could have on the brain and nervous system that might cause someone to be vulnerable to the effects of stress and to further identify the mechanism by which the stress would have this effect.

They argue that in dopamine transmission some people have genetic abnormalities, which create a vulnerability to develop schizophrenia but on their own are not enough to produce the very severe symptoms seen in those diagnosed with schizophrenia. They also note that those with schizophrenia have higher levels of cortisol than non-sufferers, suggesting that it is these high levels of cortisol that increase the severity of the symptoms. It is their contention that it is the physiological stress response (HPA axis) that leads to the increased levels of cortisol and that, as the genetic abnormalities in dopamine are particularly affected by these high levels of cortisol, it is the combination of the two that leads to the severe symptoms of schizophrenia. As the physiological stress response can be triggered by environmental stressors, we can see the connection between the biological diathesis and environmental stress in this new neural version of the diathesis–stress model.

Question time

What is the cause of schizophrenia according to this approach?

What makes some people vulnerable to the condition?

What are the triggers that cause schizophrenia to be activated in those that are vulnerable?

The consequences of this model for the treatment of schizophrenia, combining drugs with psychological therapies

In Chapter 6, the importance of taking a more interactionist approach was noted by looking at combining the use of cognitive behaviour therapy (CBT) and family therapy with the use of drugs. The evidence presented so far in this chapter only serves to push that process further by suggesting that schizophrenia comes about due to a combination of psychological and biological factors, leading to the inevitable conclusion that the treatment should also combine these factors. However, there are still some negative reactions to the use of interactionist methods in the treatment of schizophrenia, with some arguing that the benefits may have been 'oversold' (Jauhar et al., 2014).

In a review of the use of CBT in combination with drugs, Thase et al. (2014) found a significant argument for the use of CBT and argued that a more open approach to the use of methods other than drugs can bring significant improvements in patients, particularly in helping them to understand the disturbing nature of delusions and hallucinations.

Unfortunately, the negative reaction to the use of interactionist approaches has, at least partially, been affected by the use of arguments about the influence of family members on schizophrenia, such as Meehl's argument about the schizophrenogenic mother. Johnston (2013) suggested that the idea of the schizophrenogenic mother and the subsequent rejection of it following a number of studies and research may have caused a further negative implication. She suggested that modern psychiatrists have been so haunted by the fear of suffering similar embarrassment that they have become afraid to consider the role of social situations and the family (and the mother in particular) as part of the onset of schizophrenia. According to Johnston, this was partly shown by the increasing reliance on drug treatments alone in the treatment of severe mental disorders. She cites research suggesting that between 1998 and 2007, the number of people being given drug treatment alone rose by 13 per cent.

It seems as though an interactionist approach can lead to improvements in functioning for patients with schizophrenia, as long as a more positive approach to the use of other treatments alongside drugs is adopted. However, it seems unlikely that the use of such methods on their own will be enough to provide an effective treatment.

Question time

How should we treat schizophrenia according to this approach?

Why might it be difficult to put this approach into practice?

Mini plenary

Complete the table with examples of both diathesis and stress in relation to schizophrenia.

Diathesis	Stress

AO2 (Application of knowledge): How does this apply in practice?

Interleave me now

Holism and reductionism revisited

The holism–reductionism debate is one of those debates that comes down to whether you want to look for the simplest explanation for something or the most complex explanation. The simplest explanation would seek to find a single cause for examples of behaviour so that we could test that explanation more easily, that is reductionism. Whereas, the most complex explanation would try to look at the complete picture to explain behaviour and explore all of the factors that might influence it, that is holism.

Holism and reductionism in the treatment of schizophrenia

As seen in Chapter 4, an important consideration in our understanding of mental disorders should be the extent to which we are providing a holistic or reductionist view and the likely implications of that for treatment. This debate is important for the treatment of mental disorders as both sides can potentially bring benefits and make the treatment more effective.

The traditional view of psychiatry with regard to mental disorders has been that they should be treated like any other branch of medicine with medical interventions that mostly rely on the use of drugs. This has been exacerbated in the treatment of schizophrenia by the difficulty of using other non-drug methods, as patients may have a lack of insight into their disorder and be so confused by their symptoms that it is hard to make inroads into their psyche, therefore making psychological methods extremely difficult to apply.

Roache (2019) argued that it is important for psychiatry to recognise that sticking only to biological approaches may involve a level of reductionism that makes the treatment of mental disorders like schizophrenia ineffective. She suggested that a broader approach involving a combination of biological, psychological and social factors and their associated treatments may help to bring about a change in the effectiveness of treatment. This is particularly true if the social factors are better understood, as it is these that are most often ignored, not least because they are the ones that are the most difficult to pin down in terms of which factors may be relevant to mental health.

It may be that a more holistic approach to treating schizophrenia is desirable in the long-term, however Ghaemi (2009) has argued that suggesting that we take a more eclectic approach to treatment simply because it seems like we should runs the risk of creating the same kind dogma that the biological approach is being accused of. He suggests that if we just argue that more is better, we may end up not providing the most effective treatment in either the short term or the long term.

Think!

Is a holist approach or reductionist approach better when treating schizophrenia?

Why do scientists believe in the value of reductionism?

Is it possible to just accept one way or the other, or is there a middle way?

Interleave me now

The fight-or-flight response

Imagine you are walking down the street and you encounter a bear walking towards you on your side of the street, what would you do? Would you run away or would you hope that the bear will ignore you, or would you decide to fight it out and hope that you could defeat the bear in a straight fight. To be honest, none of these responses is likely to get you very far, as the bear can run faster than you and you certainly couldn't beat it in a fight, so you might be better hoping that ignoring it will work. Nonetheless, your body is likely to react in way that will prepare you for the other two options, just in case, and this is called the fight-or-flight response.

The fight-or-flight response is an example of the central nervous system and the endocrine system working together to produce a response to a stressful event that will hopefully enable us to survive. Unlike the example outlined above, we would have to imagine ourselves in a more natural situation than the one outlined above, however, stressful situations can occur in more normal, day-to-day situations and can trigger a similar response, e.g. exam stress.

This response is triggered in response to acute stress and involves the auto-nomic nervous system changing from its resting, parasympathetic state to its aroused, sympathetic state. At the same time adrenaline is released from the adrenal medulla, which is a part of the adrenal gland, and this activation leads to a number of physiological changes that will result in the increased possibility of fight or flight.

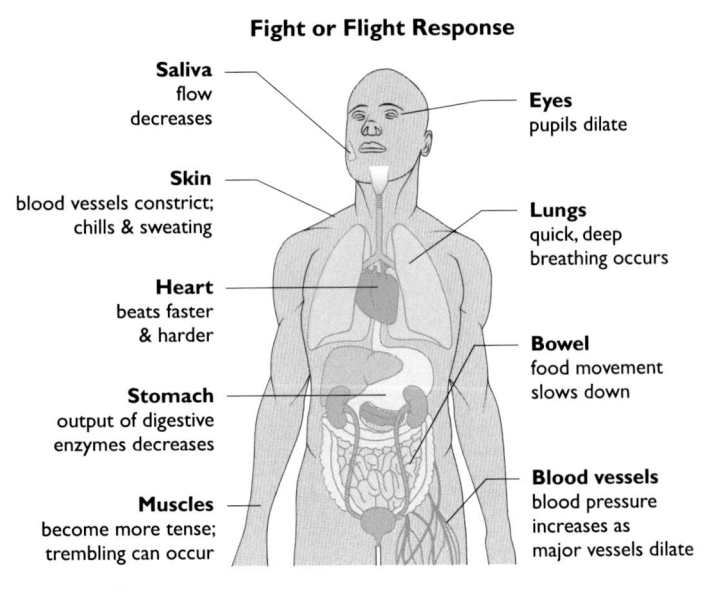

Fight or Flight Response

Saliva
flow decreases

Eyes
pupils dilate

Skin
blood vessels constrict;
chills & sweating

Lungs
quick, deep
breathing occurs

Heart
beats faster
& harder

Bowel
food movement
slows down

Stomach
output of digestive
enzymes decreases

Blood vessels
blood pressure
increases as
major vessels dilate

Muscles
become more tense;
trembling can occur

Figure 7.1 The fight-or-flight response

The HPA axis

The fight-or-flight response above is activated in response to acute, short-term stress that will hopefully end as quickly as it began, leading to the return of the autonomic nervous system to its resting, parasympathetic state.

However, sometimes we suffer chronic stress due to the fact that some stressors are long term, and this leads to a different and sometimes quite damaging response that involves the HPA axis. The HPA, short for the hypothalamic-pituitary adrenal system, is activated in much the same way as the fight-or-flight response after the hypothalamus is activated, but this time in response to stressors that occur over a long period of time, e.g. long-term abuse. Activation in the hypothalamus triggers the release of a hormone called CRF, which stimulates the pituitary gland to release adrenocorticotropic hormone (ACTH). In turn this activates the adrenal cortex to release the stress hormone cortisol. Cortisol has positive effects in this process as it helps to maintain a steady supply of blood sugar, which helps the body to cope with stress. However, it also has negative effects in the long term as it suppresses the immune system, exposing the body to a greater chance of infection.

In the neural diathesis–stress model of schizophrenia, Walker and Difioro have identified the HPA axis as an important factor in the development of schizophrenia as the high levels of cortisol produced by prolonged stress are a significant influence on the development of schizophrenia. This notion that it is long-term stressors like abuse that act as the catalyst for the development of schizophrenia in those with a genetic vulnerability shows how and why interactionist approaches are so important in explaining schizophrenia.

Question time

What does this tell us about the cause of schizophrenia?

Doesn't this show that ultimately everything is simply biological, and our biology will determine our responses to everything?

Mini plenary

Studies have shown that some people have a gene that influences the development of schizophrenia, but that not everyone with the gene actually develops the disorder.

Explain these findings with reference to the diathesis–stress model of schizophrenia?

AO3 (Analysis and evaluation of knowledge): How useful is this approach?

What is the evidence for the interactionist approach?

A constant problem for any approach that attempts to argue that genes play a role in the development of a mental disorder is separating off the influence of genes from the influence of the environment. This is particularly problematic when attempting to argue that both play a part, as this approach does, because it is hard to isolate the effect of one from the other in order to show that schizophrenia doesn't develop in the absence of one or the other. However, Tienari et al. (2004) were able to overcome this problem by investigating the effect on people with schizophrenia in adopted families. This method enables the genetic influence to be separated from the environmental influence, so that we can show how genes and environment interact when studying the development of schizophrenia.

Tienari et al. studied children adopted from over 19,000 Finnish mothers who had a history of psychosis so that they could identify those with a genetic link to schizophrenia and compare them to a control group of adopted children with no genetic link to schizophrenia. They then assessed the characteristics of child rearing employed within both groups to find those who were characterised by high levels of conflict/criticism and low levels of empathy to see the effect of environmental pressures. They found that families with these characteristics were significantly more likely to have children diagnosed with schizophrenia, but only in the group with the pre-existing genetic link to schizophrenia. Furthermore, they were able to show that child-rearing styles without these characteristics were able to guard against the development of schizophrenia in their children.

This suggests that it is the combination of the genetic vulnerability and the environmental stressor of a conflicting and critical family that lead to the development of the disorder, and that one without the other doesn't have this effect. This is strong support for the interactionist view that it is the gene–environment interaction that is fundamentally important in the development of schizophrenia.

> **Think!**
>
> Why is the evidence from adoption studies more convincing than evidence from other types of family studies?

Is any type of stress enough to affect the neural diathesis–stress model?

The neural diathesis–stress model suggests that the stressors that trigger the symptoms of schizophrenia are related to the increased production of cortisol and, as such, it doesn't matter what kind of stress it, as long as it is long term and related to this cortisol effect. There is research to show this effect. Walder et al. (2000) found that high levels of cortisol were linked to the severity of the positive symptoms of schizophrenia. However, Ritsner et al. (2004) found that although increased cortisol was related to the symptoms of anxiety, anger and depression in patients with schizophrenia, they were not related to the severity of the psychotic symptoms. This contradictory evidence has led some to argue that different forms of long-term stress have different effects, and therefore it is possible that the specific form of stress may influence whether it leads to the development of schizophrenic symptoms, even in those that have such a vulnerability.

Jones and Fernyhough (2006) have argued that in healthy people cortisol production is much higher in response to forms of stress seen to be uncontrollable, and therefore impossible to avoid, and forms of stress that involve some form of negative evaluation of our abilities to perform tasks that we regard as important to us, e.g. in the workplace. They suggest that this would help to explain the contradictory research mentioned above as the neural diathesis–stress model has failed to take proper account of the effect of different forms of stress on cortisol levels and, therefore, although the theory may still be sound, it only works if we take into account the different forms of stress.

This suggests that the HPA axis and the development of cortisol may well be key to understanding the severity of symptoms in those with schizophrenia, and the theory may well show the interaction between that and the vulnerability caused by abnormalities in dopamine transmission. However, the theory assumes that all forms of stress are the same and are sufficient to trigger the response, when in fact it is likely that an understanding that only certain forms of stress will produce this response is needed if we are going to make a valid contribution to the discussion.

Furthermore, Jones and Fernyhough argue that an understanding of this sort has important implications for treatment, as vulnerable individuals may perceive both uncontrollability and negative self-evaluation in situations that don't pose that kind of threat and, as such, the best way to deal with this would be to use CBT to help them understand the nature of the threat more clearly. This is particularly important as it seems that antipsychotics are less effective in this area.

> **Think!**
>
> Are there any forms of stress that are controllable?
> Is stress always a bad thing?

What is the evidence for the effectiveness of interactionist treatments?

As seen in previous chapters, there is evidence for both the use of psychological therapies and drug treatments in treating schizophrenia and both are currently being used to treat the disorder to varying degrees across the world. However, it is necessary to consider the effectiveness of these kind of treatments as it may or may not be cost-effective to launch into a wide-ranging roll-out of the use of these approaches without understanding their efficacy.

From an interactionist perspective, it would be assumed that a combined approach of psychological treatments and drugs would be more effective than drugs alone. Tarrier et al. (2004) studied this hypothesis with over 300 patients from 11 mental health units in the UK, who were assigned to a medication alone group, a CBT-plus-medication group and a supportive counselling-plus-medication group. All patients were assessed after 18 months on symptom improvement and relapse rates. They found a significant difference between the two combined groups and the medication-alone group, such that the two combined groups showed significantly greater improvement in symptoms than the medication-alone group, although there was significant difference in relapse rates between the three groups. This suggests that a combined approach is superior, providing significant support for the interactionist approach to treatment.

However, in a study comparing the effectiveness of CBT alone, antipsychotics alone and a combination of CBT and antipsychotics, Morrison et al. (2018) found that although the combined approach led to a significant improvement in symptoms compared to the CBT-alone group, there was no significant difference between the combined group and the antipsychotics-alone group. This suggests that although a combined approach is better than CBT alone in terms of effectiveness, there is no such evidence for the effectiveness of an interactionist approach to treatment compared to the use of drugs alone. Furthermore, there were significantly fewer side effects in the CBT-alone group, which further confounds the issue of which approach is the more suitable – as the combined approach still exposes patients to potentially severe side effects.

> **Think!**
>
> Should we always adopt an interactionist approach when treating all mental disorders?
>
> What are the practical problems with doing that?

What is the treatment-causation fallacy?

There seems to be some evidence to suggest that an interactionist approach to treatment is beneficial, and this might therefore support the view that the interactionist approach to the cause of schizophrenia might also have some merit. If interactionist treatment works, then we might reasonably suppose that it is the combination of factors that causes the development of schizophrenia in the first place. However, we have also seen above and in previous chapters that medication alone and psychological therapies alone also have some evidence of effectiveness and therefore, it might be just as reasonable to assume that that it is these factors alone that lead to the development of the disorder. Unfortunately, this is an example of what is called the treatment-causation fallacy.

This problem arises from our tendency to believe that if we make some kind of intervention into a problem that we have, which is subsequently successful, then the cause of that problem must in some way be related to what we did to solve the problem. This has been a particular problem for biological interventions; for example the finding that drugs that block the production of dopamine and are successful in treating schizophrenia must lead to the dopamine hypothesis. After all, if we treat someone with dopamine antagonists and they get better, then it must be the case that it was the dopamine that was causing the problem in the first place, right? Not really, because that would be like saying that if we have a headache and we take paracetamol and then it gets better, our headache must have been caused by a lack of paracetamol, which seems pretty unlikely. Although, it might be more reasonable to say that the headache was caused by dehydration and the water that we took with the paracetamol lessened that, in which case the treatment-causation idea works!

This kind of fallacy can also be seen clearly from psychological therapies too. For example, could we argue that the effectiveness of counselling or CBT means that schizophrenia was caused by a lack of counselling or CBT. In relation to interactionist approaches, this fallacy becomes even more evident as we are now looking at more than one treatment, making it even harder to say that it is one thing or another that causes the development of schizophrenia, although, if we adopt the view that there are multiple causes, then maybe the interactionist approach is proven right.

Unfortunately, the problem remains and can be seen quite clearly by anyone who is or has in the past been involved in bringing up children. Could we say that, when a child cries and we give that child something sweet such as a lollipop and they stop crying, their crying was caused by the lack of a lollipop? Clearly not.

Question time

What are the benefits of an interactionist approach to understanding the development and treatment of schizophrenia?

Are these claimed benefits justified by the evidence?

What are the problems of adopting an interactionist approach to the treatment of schizophrenia?

Mini plenary

Using the evaluation points above, try to identify arguments for and against the following statement.

An interactionist approach is the only way to understand and treat schizophrenia.

Arguments for	Arguments against

INTERACTIONIST APPROACH TO SCHIZOPHRENIA

The use of modern techniques to identify schizophrenia has the potential to improve the diagnosis of schizophrenia as it becomes less subjective, but it may also create problems, as it takes professional judgement away from the doctor and puts it in the hands of a machine. It may also have the potential of labelling anyone with certain brain differences as abnormal even though they may be fine.

New research

CLINICAL PSYCHIATRY NEWS

Brain mapping takes next step toward precision psychiatry

Heidi Splete

10 October 2018

In this article the use of brain mapping is discussed based around the idea that psychiatry is one area of medicine that still diagnoses disorders on the basis of symptoms alone. Splete argues that there is evidence from research that suggests that a more scientific approach could be adopted with the use of brain mapping to help identify the risk of schizophrenia development.

Splete refers to research conducted by the Radboud University in the Netherlands in which Thomas Wolfers and his colleagues used brain scans and mapping models with 163 adults with schizophrenia and 190 adults with bipolar disorder to compare to 256 healthy adults in a control group.

The study was based around the idea that those with schizophrenia have significant homogeneity in their brain structure, which should help to identify brain markers in those with schizophrenia that could be used in the future to reliably identify those with or even at risk of developing schizophrenia. Such homogeneity would be particularly useful to the medical profession as they would no longer have to rely on subjective diagnoses when assessing patients who might present with the symptoms of a psychotic disorder.

Unfortunately, Wolfers and his colleagues were unable to identify obvious structural differences between the patients and the controls, such that similar deviations were evident in less than 2 per cent of the sample of those with schizophrenia. This suggests that schizophrenia and bipolar disorder are examples of 'highly heterogenous mental disorders'.

Furthermore, the researchers were unable to control for any confounding variables and were therefore unable to make any reliable conclusions about the causes of schizophrenia.

GLOSSARY

Question time

What does this article tell us about the causes of schizophrenia?

What does this suggest about the interactionist approach to schizophrenia?

What might be the implications of identifying brain abnormalities as the cause of schizophrenia?

Chapter plenary

1. What is an interactionist approach?
2. What is the diathesis–stress model of schizophrenia?
3. How has the idea of diathesis changed in relation to schizophrenia?
4. How has the idea of stress changed in relation to schizophrenia?
5. What is the neural diathesis–stress model of schizophrenia?
6. What are the consequences of this model for the treatment of schizophrenia?
7. What is the holism–reductionism debate?
8. How does the holism–reductionism debate apply to the treatment of schizophrenia?
9. What is the fight-or-flight response?
10. What is the HPA axis?
11. What is the evidence for the interactionist approach in relation to explaining schizophrenia?
12. Is any type of stress enough to affect the neural diathesis–stress model of schizophrenia?
13. What is the evidence for the effectiveness of interactionist treatments?
14. What is the treatment-causation fallacy?
15. Is brain-mapping a useful tool in psychiatry?

Glossary

Key word	Definition
Adrenal cortex	The outer part of the adrenal gland, located on top of each kidney. It produces hormones that are vital to life, such as cortisol and aldosterone (which helps control blood pressure).
Adrenal medulla	The inner part of the adrenal gland that controls the hormones involved in the fight or flight response, e.g. adrenaline.
Adrenaline	A hormone produced by the adrenal glands that increases physiological arousal by increasing blood circulation, breathing and metabolic rate.

Key word	Definition
Adrenocorticotropic hormone (ACTH)	A hormone produced by the pituitary gland that helps to regulate the production of cortisol by the adrenal glands.
Cortisol	Known as the stress hormone as it is released during stress but has many important functions, including maintaining a steady supply of blood sugar.
CRF	Stands for corticotropin-releasing factor and is a hormone that stimulates the pituitary gland to release ACTH.
Diathesis	A medical term that refers to the idea of being predisposed to a particular physical state or disorder.
Fight-or-flight response	A physiological response that occurs when we feel threatened or in danger.
Holist	The most complex explanation that tries to look at the complete picture to explain behaviour and explore all of the factors that might influence it.
HPA axis	A term used to describe the system that connects the hypothalamus, pituitary gland and adrenal glands as part of the stress response.
Hypothalamus	Part of the brain that coordinates the activity of the autonomic nervous system and the pituitary gland. It helps to maintain balance in bodily functions.
Interactionism	An approach to explaining the phenomenon that combines two or more types of information, usually biological and psychological/social.
Parasympathetic state	The resting state that occurs when the autonomic nervous system is conserving energy.
Pituitary gland	The master gland that is located in the brain and controls the functions of the other glands in the endocrine system.
Reductionist	The simplest explanation that seeks to find a single cause for behaviour.
Schizophrenogenic mother	A negative stereotype developed by Fromm-Reichman (1948) to describe a mother who is domineering, cold and rejecting, which causes their child to develop schizophrenia.
Stress	In this context, it refers to any event that may create the feeling of a threat or place demands on you that you feel you need to respond to.
Sympathetic state	The aroused state that occurs when the autonomic nervous system needs to respond to a perceived threat.
Treatment-causation fallacy	The erroneous belief that if a treatment is effective then the cause of the problem must be whatever was targeted by the treatment.

Question 1.

Outline the diathesis–stress model of schizophrenia. [4 marks]

Marks for this question: AO1 = 4

Advice: In a question like this, it's important to make sure you are clearly explaining the model in relation to schizophrenia, rather than just identifying/outlining what is meant by diathesis and stress. The other issue with a question like this is the tendency to do too much, as there are many points that you could make. So it's important to remain concise in your answer. There is no need to provide any analysis or evaluation as all of the marks are for AO1: Knowledge and understanding.

Possible answer: The diathesis–stress model is part of the interactionist approach to explaining mental disorders and suggests that schizophrenia is caused by a combination of biological and psychological/social factors. In the original model, the suggestion was that the diathesis was a genetic vulnerability that would make someone predisposed to develop schizophrenia, but that without the environmental stress alongside it then the disorder wouldn't develop. In the original model, the stress factor was believed to be caused by the presence of a schizophrenogenic mother in the life of a child/young person. However, new versions of this model have suggested that the vulnerability to develop the disorder could be related to traumatic events in childhood and that the stress could be related to the introduction of chemicals into a person's system that trigger the disorder, particularly the use of cannabis. The diathesis part indicates that some people have a vulnerability to develop schizophrenia and in the original model this was based on a genetic vulnerability.

Question 2.

Describe and evaluate the interactionist approach to explaining and treating schizophrenia. [16 marks]

Marks for this question: AO1 = 6 and AO3 = 10

Advice: This question is looking both for skills of knowledge and understanding and for skills of analysis and evaluation. It should be noted that the question asks about both explaining and treating and although they don't have to be perfectly balanced, it is necessary to provide sufficient material on each to achieve higher levels. As there are 6 marks for AO1 and 10 for AO3, there should be greater emphasis on the evaluation. However, all such extended writing questions are marked holistically and therefore it is important that the knowledge is accurate and detailed, and that the evaluation is clear and effective.

Possible answer: The interactionist approach to schizophrenia is based around the idea that it isn't possible to explain or treat the disorder without incorporating both biological and psychological factors into the explanation of causes and the proposed treatment. The diathesis–stress model has been used to explain how some people have a genetic vulnerability that makes them predisposed to develop schizophrenia, although that it wouldn't actually happen without it being triggered by some form of environmental stress.

In Meehl's original model, the diathesis or predisposition was believed to be a genetic vulnerability and the stress was believed to be the presence of a schizophrenogenic mother in the life of a child/young person. However, new versions of the model have incorporated the idea of traumatic experiences creating a vulnerability and the introduction of chemicals such as cannabis in later life as the trigger. So while there is still the notion that it involves a combination of biological and psychological/social factors in the development of the disorder, it is less rigid in the belief of which one is the diathesis and which is the stress. This model has been further modified in recent times in the neural diathesis–stress model to provide more detail on how these factors combine to produce schizophrenia.

According to Walker and Diforio, the genetic part relates to abnormalities in the transmission of dopamine, which, unlike the biological approach, isn't enough on its own to explain schizophrenia, but when combined with the increased levels of cortisol that come about as part of the physiological response to long-term stress create the perfect conditions to bring about schizophrenia. As the long-term stress is likely to be caused by environmental factors, we can see how biology and environment combine to produce schizophrenia.

Interactionist treatments recognise the need to deal with the biological effects of schizophrenia, such as the high levels of dopamine, but also recognise the need to deal with the stress factors that could trigger the response. Therefore, the approach looks at a combination of antipsychotic drugs that block dopamine with psychological approaches such as CBT, counselling and family therapy, which can help to restructure someone's understanding of the environmental stressors affecting them. CBT can help a person come to terms with the delusions and hallucinations that are typical symptoms of schizophrenia through the use of techniques to challenge the reality of these symptoms. Family therapy can be used to create an environment where the environmental stressors are less likely to be a continuous threat to a person's recovery.

This holistic approach to explaining and treating schizophrenia has potential benefits as it is attempting to deal with the complete picture, rather than just a section of it that might come about from just using drugs. However, being unable to identify a single cause may create problems, as the stressor could be a whole range of factors that are triggering the disorder, whereas the only thing we can be sure of is that the person has raised dopamine levels and we have drugs to treat that. It has also been noted that some people with schizophrenia don't have raised dopamine levels and that some of the symptoms are related to low dopamine levels or completely different neurotransmitters, so possibly a reductionist approach isn't so useful after all.

There is some evidence of the interactionist approach to explaining schizophrenia as Tienari et al. conducted a study of children adopted from over

19,000 Finnish mothers with a history of psychotic disturbance in order to identify children who may have a genetic link to schizophrenia. They also studied a group of adopted children with no genetic link to schizophrenia to act as a control group. They studied the child-rearing styles used with both groups and found that those with a genetic link were more likely to develop schizophrenia but only if they had the added issue of a child-rearing style that was high in conflict and criticism, suggesting that it was the combination of the two that led to schizophrenia and therefore that the interactionist approach is correct.

Walker and Difioro's neural model has advanced our understanding of how chronic stress may cause a physiological response that affects genetic vulnerability and therefore it could be any form of stress that acts as the trigger for schizophrenia. However, some researchers have argued that not all forms of stress have the same effect and that it is only certain forms of stress that have this effect on the HPA axis. Jones and Fernyhough have argued that in healthy people cortisol production is much higher in response to forms of stress that are seen to be uncontrollable and involve some form of negative evaluation of abilities that are important to us, and therefore only these forms of stress would be relevant to this new model. So, the theory only works if we take into account the different forms of stress.

Evidence for interactionist treatments comes from Tarrier et al. who compared a group given drugs alone to treat schizophrenia with groups being given either CBT-plus-drugs or supportive counselling-plus-drugs and found that the combined groups both improved more than the drugs-alone group. However, Morrison et al. compared groups using drugs alone, CBT alone and a combination of drugs and CBT, and even though they found that the combined group improved more than the CBT-alone group, there was no significant difference between the combined group and the drugs-alone group. This suggests that it may be difficult to treat schizophrenia without the use of drugs and if drugs alone can perform equally well, it may not be worth the expense of using other treatments.

A further problem that arises from all treatments used with schizophrenia is whether or not we can infer the cause from successful treatments. It would be nice to think that if a treatment works, then we can say that the cause must be related to whatever we did to treat the problem. This is sometimes referred to as the treatment-causation fallacy. This is an error that comes about from our desire to believe that what makes you better is likely to be related to whatever caused the problem in the first place, so, for example, if interactionist treatments work then it must be the same combination that caused the problem. However, this is like saying that if we take paracetamol for a headache and the headache goes that it must have been the lack of paracetamol that caused the problem, which is, of course, ridiculous. Unfortunately, probably the best we can do at the moment is to consider whether drug treatments work and if they do, and there are few side effects, then we can say that they are an effective treatment regardless of the actual cause of the disorder.

References

Fromm-Reichman, F. (1948) Notes on the development treatment of schizophrenia by psychoanalytic psychotherapy. *Psychiatry*, 11: 263–273.

Ghaemi, S.N. (2009) The rise and fall of the biopsychosocial model. *The British Journal of Psychiatry*, 195 (1): 3–4.

Houston, J.E., Murphy, J., Adamson, G., Stringer, M. and Shevlin, M. (2007) Childhood sexual abuse, early cannabis use, and psychosis: Testing an interaction model based on the National Comorbidity Survey. *Schizophrenia Bulletin*, 34 (3): 580–585.

Jauhar, S., McKenna, P.J., Radua, J., Fung, E., Salvador, R. and Laws, K.R. (2014) Cognitive–behavioural therapy for the symptoms of schizophrenia: Systematic review and meta-analysis with examination of potential bias. *The British Journal of Psychiatry*, 204 (1): 20–29.

Johnston, J. (2013) The ghost of the schizophrenogenic mother. *AMA Journal of Ethics*, 15 (9): 801–805.

Jones, S.R. and Fernyhough, C. (2006). A new look at the neural diathesis–stress model of schizophrenia: The primacy of social-evaluative and uncontrollable situations. *Schizophrenia Bulletin*, 33 (5): 1171–1177.

Meehl, P.E. (1962) Schizotaxia, schizotypy, schizophrenia. *American Psychologist*, 17: 827–838.

Morrison, A.P., Law, H., Carter, L., Sellers, R., Emsley, R., Pyle, M., French, P., Shiers, D., Yung, A.R., Murphy, E.K. and Holden, N. (2018) Antipsychotic drugs versus cognitive behavioural therapy versus a combination of both in people with psychosis: A randomised controlled pilot and feasibility study. *The Lancet Psychiatry*, 5 (5): 411–423.

Read, J., Perry, B.D., Moskowitz, A. and Connolly, J. (2001) The contribution of early traumatic events to schizophrenia in some patients: A traumagenic neurodevelopmental model. *Psychiatry: Interpersonal and Biological Processes*, 64 (4): 319–345.

Ritsner, M., Maayan, R., Gibel, A., Strous, R.D., Modai, I. and Weizman, A. (2004) Elevation of the cortisol/dehydroepiandrosterone ratio in schizophrenia patients. *European Neuropsychopharmacology*, 14 (4): 267–273.

Roache, R. (2019). Psychiatry's problem with reductionism. *Philosophy, Psychiatry, & Psychology*, 26 (3): 219–229.

Splete, H. (2018) Brain mapping takes next step toward precision psychiatry. *Clinical Psychiatry News*, 10 October 2018.

Tarrier, N., Lewis, S., Haddock, G., Bentall, R., Drake, R., Kinderman, P., Kingdon, D., Siddle, R. Everitt, J., Leadley, K. and Benn, A. (2004) Cognitive–behavioural therapy in first episode and early schizophrenia: 18-month follow-up of a randomised controlled trial. *The British Journal of Psychiatry*, 184 (3): 231–239.

Thase, M.E., Kingdon, D. and Turkington, D. (2014) The promise of cognitive behavior therapy for treatment of severe mental disorders: A review of recent developments. *World Psychiatry*, 13 (3): 244–250.

Tienari, P., Wynne, L.C., Sorri, A., Lahti, I., Läksy, K., Moring, J., Naarala, M., Nieminen, P. and Wahlberg, K.E. (2004) Genotype–environment interaction in schizophrenia-spectrum disorder: Long-term follow-up study of Finnish adoptees. *The British Journal of Psychiatry*, 184 (3): 216–222.

Walder, D.J., Walker, E.F. and Lewine, R.J. (2000). Cognitive functioning, cortisol release, and symptom severity in patients with schizophrenia. *Biological Psychiatry*, 48 (12): 1121–1132.

Walker, E.F. and Diforio, D. (1997) Schizophrenia: A neural diathesis–stress model. *Psychological Review*, 104 (4): 667.

Index